The No Nonsense Boundaries in Marriage Workbook

Enhance Intimacy and Respect with Proven Techniques to Build Trust, Communication, and a Harmonious Partnership

Jeffrey C. Chapman

Copyright © [Year of First Publication] by [Author or Pen Name]

All rights reserved.

No portion of this book may be reproduced in any form without written permission from the publisher or author, except as permitted by U.S. copyright law.

This publication is designed to provide accurate and authoritative information in regard to the subject matter covered. It is sold with the understanding that neither the author nor the publisher is engaged in rendering legal, investment, accounting or other professional services. While the publisher and author have used their best efforts in preparing this book, they make no representations or warranties with respect to the accuracy or completeness of the contents of this book and specifically disclaim any implied warranties of merchantability or fitness for a particular purpose. No warranty may be created or extended by sales representatives or written sales materials. The advice and strategies contained herein may not be suitable for your situation. You should consult with a professional when appropriate. Neither the publisher nor the author shall be liable for any loss of profit or any other commercial damages, including but not limited to special, incidental, consequential, personal, or other damages.

Book Cover by [Artist]

Illustrations by [Illustrator]

[Edition Number] edition [Year of Publication]

CONTENTS

Introduction: Boundaries—Not Boring, Just Brilliant

What if I told you that the secret to a thriving, passionate marriage isn't grand romantic gestures or lavish date nights, but something far simpler? What if the key to keeping the spark alive is... boundaries?

I know, I know. "Boundaries" don't exactly scream fun and sexy. You might be picturing a stern lecture or a rigid list of rules. But stick with me—boundaries are the unsung heroes of a healthy relationship. They create a framework of mutual respect, trust, and understanding. Inside that framework, love can actually flourish.

Think of boundaries like the walls of your house. Sure, walls might seem restrictive at first glance, but they create a safe, intimate space. They give you the freedom to relax, to be yourself, to dance around in your underwear if you want to. Boundaries in marriage do the same thing. By defining what's okay and what's not, you create the security needed for your relationship to thrive.

So, let's toss the old misconceptions aside. Boundaries aren't stiff or sterile; they're the secret sauce to a lasting, joyful marriage. As you move through this book, you'll learn how to build boundaries with joy, humor, and heart. You'll see how clear limits make space for laughter, affection, and even spontaneity.

Workbook Exercise: Boundary Busters Journal

Before we dive into building better boundaries, let's reflect on your relationship with them. Grab a pen and a notebook and get real.

What comes to mind when you hear the word "boundaries"? Jot down the first few words or phrases that pop into your head. Now, think about your own marriage or relationship. What myths or misconceptions have you bought into? Have you thought of boundaries as cold, rigid, or unromantic? Write down any negative associations you have.

Next, consider how those beliefs have impacted your relationship. Have you avoided setting boundaries out of fear they'd kill the spark? Or maybe you've found yourself feeling resentful or overwhelmed because your needs aren't being met. Write down a few examples.

Now, let's reframe. What would your relationship look like if you saw boundaries as a positive, loving tool? What if clear limits created more room for intimacy, trust, and joy? Write down a few potential benefits of healthy boundaries in your marriage.

Finally, set an intention. As you move through this book, what do you want to learn or change about the way you approach boundaries? What's your top goal or priority?

Remember, there are no right or wrong answers here. The purpose of this exercise is simply to raise your awareness and start shifting your mindset. Keep your journal handy as we continue—we'll be doing plenty of reflection and discovery along the way!

PART I: FIRST, FIX YOUR FOUNDATIONS

CHAPTER ONE

How to Reboot a Relationship Without Making It Weird

Ever wish there was a "reset" button for your relationship? A way to wipe the slate clean and start fresh? While you won't find an actual button to press, there are steps you can take to give your marriage a much-needed reboot—no awkwardness required.

The Power of Hitting Reset

Think about your computer. When it starts acting glitchy or running slowly, what's the first thing you do? You restart it, letting it clear out the glitches and run smoothly again.

Your marriage is similar. Over time, you and your partner might fall into patterns that no longer serve you—maybe snapping at each other over small things, or letting date night fall by the wayside. These habits can make your relationship feel sluggish, like a computer overdue for a reset.

Dr. John Gottman, a psychologist and relationship expert, identifies four negative patterns that often creep into relationships: criticism, contempt, defensiveness, and stonewalling. He calls them the "Four Horsemen of the Apocalypse"[1]. When these behaviors take over, relationship satisfaction drops, sometimes leading to separation or divorce.

Hitting reset doesn't mean erasing your history or pretending problems don't exist. Instead, it's about making a conscious choice to let go of built-up resentments, recommit to your shared values, and make space for healthier patterns to take root.

The key to resetting is "turning toward" each other. Dr. Gottman's research shows that couples who regularly respond to each other's bids for connection—small moments of reaching out—have happier, more stable relationships (Gottman & Silver, 1999). By pressing reset, you're choosing to turn toward each other with renewed openness and intentionality.

$$\cdot \; \cdot \; \cdot \; \bullet \; \cdot \; \bullet \; \bullet \; \cdot \; \cdot$$

The Science of Relationship Resets

Resetting isn't just a feel-good concept—it's grounded in science. Research shows that engaging in new, exciting activities together can boost relationship satisfaction and intimacy[2]. Novel experiences trigger the brain's reward system, flooding it with feel-good chemicals like dopamine[3]. By breaking your routine and trying new things as a couple, you create positive memories and associate that excitement with your partner, rekindling closeness and passion.

Another critical piece is habit formation. It takes, on average, 66 days to form a new habit[4]. By consciously practicing new ways of interacting—like expressing gratitude or having regular check-ins—you can turn these behaviors into automatic habits that support the long-term health of your relationship.

That said, hitting reset isn't always easy. It requires vulnerability, effort, and a willingness to step outside your comfort zone. There will be moments of resistance or discomfort as you adopt new ways of being together.

This is where the concept of "rupture and repair" comes in. Dr. Sue Johnson, a relationship researcher, explains that the strength of a relationship isn't in the absence of conflict but in the ability to repair after a rupture.[5] A reset may involve moments of frustration or even conflict, but these moments are opportunities to strengthen your bond by practicing repair and reconnection.

$$\bullet \; \bullet \; \bullet \; \bullet \; \bullet \; \bullet \; \bullet \; \bullet \; \bullet \; \bullet$$

How to Reboot with Respect

So, how do you hit reset in a way that feels collaborative, not threatening? Here are some key steps:

1. **Start with Self-Reflection**

   Before you initiate a reset with your partner, take time to reflect on your own behavior. Consider:

   - What patterns might I be contributing to?

   - How can I show up as my best self in this partnership?

   - What are my intentions for this reset?

2. **Invite, Don't Impose**

   Frame the reset as an invitation to collaborate. Use "I" statements to share your feelings and desires, and ask open-ended questions to understand your partner's perspective. For example:

   - "I've been reflecting a lot on our relationship recently, and I'm realizing how much I want us to feel close and connected again. I'm wondering if you'd be open to discussing the idea of intentionally starting fresh together?"

   - "I know we've fallen into some patterns that aren't serving us well. I'm committed to working on my part, and I'm curious to hear your thoughts on how we might approach this as a team. What are your hopes for our relationship moving forward?" Remember, the goal is to come to a shared understanding and agreement, not to pressure or persuade.

3. **Create a Shared Vision**

Once you're both on board, envision your "new normal" together. Ask yourselves:

- What did we love about our relationship in the beginning?

- What new qualities or experiences do we want to cultivate?

- How can we show up as our best selves, both individually and together?

4. **Start Small and Specific**

Big changes aren't necessary to reboot your relationship. Start with small, specific habits—like a daily gratitude ritual or a weekly adventure date. Research shows that small shifts lead to lasting transformation[6].

5. **Seek Support**

You don't have to do this alone. Consider seeking the guidance of a therapist or relationship coach, or engage with relationship resources like books, workshops, or online courses. Surround yourselves with positive examples that inspire your vision for your relationship.

· · · · ● · ● ● · · ·

Real-Life Reboots: Stories of Couples Who Hit Reset

Casey and Taylor's Story:

Casey and Taylor had been together for five years, but the spark had dimmed. They found themselves constantly bickering over small things, living more like roommates than partners. After one particularly frustrating argument about household chores, Casey said, "Taylor, I miss us. I miss the way we used to laugh together. We can't go back in time, but what if we could start fresh and make us a priority again?" Taylor agreed, and over the following weeks, they committed to intentional conversations and small changes. They started a nightly gratitude practice, scheduled bi-weekly date nights, and learned to take time-outs when conflicts escalated. It wasn't easy, but by approaching their challenges with compassion, Casey and Taylor gradually rediscovered their connection.

Morgan and Jordan's Reset:

Morgan and Jordan had been married for 15 years when their busy lives left little time for connection. They were more focused on logistics than intimacy. One day, Morgan came across an article about relationship reboots. Feeling hopeful, they shared it with Jordan and asked if they could give it a try. Jordan agreed. Together, they attended a couples workshop to rekindle intimacy. They instituted a "no phones" rule during dinner and in the bedroom, creating space for conversation. They also began a weekly "marriage meeting" to check in on their relationship. Slowly, Morgan and Jordan started to reconnect, building a new way of being together that honored their past but allowed for growth.

· · · · ● · ● · · · ·

Embracing the Journey

Rebooting your relationship is an act of courage and love. It's a commitment to honor your past while consciously creating your future. It's not about perfection, but about curiosity, patience, and a willingness to grow.

As you embark on this journey, celebrate your small victories and learn from the inevitable stumbles. Keep your focus on the horizon—on the relationship you're building, step by intentional step. With commitment, care, and creativity, you have the power to design a love that lasts a lifetime.

Workbook Exercise: The Reset Ritual

Step 1: Individual Reflection

Before coming together with your partner, take some time to reflect individually. In your journal or a notebook, write down your responses to the following prompts:

1. What are three habits or patterns in your relationship that you'd like to change? These could be things like arguing over petty issues, neglecting quality time together, or taking each other for granted.

2. What are three new habits or practices you'd like to cultivate in your relationship? These could be things like expressing gratitude daily, having regular check-ins, or creating shared goals.

3. How do you envision these changes improving your relationship? What do you hope your "new normal" will feel like?

Step 2: Couple Discussion

Once you've both had a chance to reflect individually, come together to share your insights. Find a quiet, comfortable space where you can talk without distractions. Take turns sharing your responses to the prompts above.

As you listen to your partner, practice active listening. Give them your full attention, and try to understand their perspective. Resist the urge to interrupt, defend, or problem-solve. Simply let them feel heard.

After you've both shared, discuss any common themes or desires that emerged. Where do your visions for your relationship align? What new habits would you both like to prioritize?

Step 3: Crafting Your Reset Ritual

Now it's time to design your unique Reset Ritual. This ritual will symbolize your commitment to starting fresh and creating positive change in your relationship. Here are some ideas to consider:

- Choose a meaningful location. Is there a spot that holds special significance for your relationship, like where you first met or got married? Consider doing your ritual there.

- Incorporate a symbolic action. This could be something like lighting a candle, planting a tree, or writing letters to each other expressing your recommitment.

- Create a verbal commitment. Write vows or promises to each other that reflect your intentions for this new chapter. Read them aloud as part of your ritual.

- Set a regular "reset" check-in. Decide on a frequency (weekly, monthly, etc.) to check in on your progress and recommit to your goals. Put these check-ins on your calendars.

Remember, your Reset Ritual is unique to you as a couple. Design it in a way that feels authentic and meaningful to you both.

Step 4: Commit and Begin

Once you've designed your Reset Ritual, it's time to put it into action. Choose a date and time to conduct your ritual and officially "hit reset" on your relationship.

After your ritual, keep your intentions front and center. Consider writing your new relationship habits somewhere you'll see them daily, like on your bathroom mirror or in your wallet. Check in with each other regularly about how you're doing in practicing these new behaviors.

And don't forget to celebrate your progress along the way! Acknowledge the small victories and the efforts you're both making to strengthen your bond.

Hitting reset is a courageous, loving act. By taking this step, you're investing in the long-term health and happiness of your relationship. Enjoy this new beginning!

---

1. (Gottman, 1999)

2. Aron et al., 2000

3. Aron et al., 2005

4. Lally et al., 2010

5. Johnson, 2008

6. Clear, 2018

CHAPTER TWO

THE COUPLE'S CODE: HOW TO BUILD YOUR OWN RELATIONSHIP RULEBOOK

Every relationship is unique, with its own set of needs, values, and challenges. Just as no two individuals are exactly alike, no two couples will have identical approaches to their partnership. This is where a *Couple's Code* comes in.

What is a Couple's Code?

A Couple's Code is a set of agreements, boundaries, and expectations that you and your partner create together. Think of it as a relationship constitution—a personalized guide that outlines the principles and practices that shape how you navigate life as a couple. It's a tangible commitment to co-creating a partnership that works for both of you.

Your Couple's Code might include agreements around:

- How you communicate, especially during conflicts

- Your commitments around quality time and intimacy

- Your approach to finances and decision-making

- Your boundaries around personal space and time

- Your roles and responsibilities in the relationship

For *Lauren and Chris*, creating a Couple's Code was transformative. As an introvert-extrovert pair, they often struggled to find the right balance between socializing and downtime. Their code allowed them to agree on attending social events together once a week, while Lauren could opt out of additional plans when she needed solitude. Chris, meanwhile, was free to go out with friends when Lauren needed time to recharge. They also prioritized a weekly "date night in," planning activities that felt comfortable for both of them. By putting these agreements in writing, Lauren and Chris didn't just avoid misunderstandings—they actively designed a relationship that met both their needs.

The Power of Putting Pen to Paper

Why write this down? Can't you just agree verbally and call it good? While verbal communication is important, there's something uniquely powerful about codifying your agreements in writing. Research shows that the simple act of writing something down increases commitment and follow-through[1]. Putting your intentions on paper transforms a passing thought into a tangible commitment.

Plus, having a written document gives you something concrete to reference and return to over time. On the inevitable days when you're tired, stressed, or tempted to fall back into old patterns, your Couple's Code serves as a compassionate reminder of the partnership you've consciously chosen.

For *Rachel and Sam*, writing their Couple's Code became a cherished ritual. As a same-sex couple navigating a world that wasn't always accepting, their code represented their united front. They wrote each agreement by hand in a beautiful journal, including promises like:

- "We will always stand united in the face of discrimination or disapproval."

- "We will make our home a sanctuary of love and acceptance."

- "We will honor each other's dreams and support each other's growth."

Each year on their anniversary, Rachel and Sam reread their Couple's Code, adding new insights as their relationship evolved. Their code wasn't just a set of rules; it was a living, breathing reflection of their ongoing journey together.

· · · ● · ● · ● · · ·

Crafting Your Code: A Step-by-Step Guide

Creating a Couple's Code doesn't have to be overwhelming. Here's a step-by-step guide to help you get started:

1. **Set the Stage**

   Choose a relaxed time and place to have an uninterrupted conversation with your partner. Whether it's a cozy evening at home or a special date night, create an atmosphere that feels meaningful—light some candles, pour your favorite beverages, and get comfortable.

2. **Reflect on Your Values**

   Individually reflect on the values that are most important to you in relationships. What qualities do you admire and aspire to embody? Write down your top values—these might include honesty, growth, playfulness, or security.

3. **Share and Listen**

   Take turns sharing your reflections. Practice deep listening without interruption. Ask curious questions to better understand your partner's perspective. Look for values that align or complement each other.

4. **Identify Needs and Desires**

   Reflect on what helps you feel loved, safe, and fulfilled. For example, one partner might need dedicated one-on-one time to feel connected, while the other might hope to approach disagreements as a team rather than adversaries. Share your hopes and desires and look for areas of common ground.

5. **Craft Your Agreements**

   Turn your shared values and needs into specific agreements. These could be
   serious commitments or playful promises—whatever feels authentic to you
   both. Examples might include:

   - "We agree to always tell the truth, even when it's difficult."

   - "We'll have a weekly adventure date where we try something new together."

   - "We'll share household responsibilities based on our strengths."

6. **Make It Official**

   Once you've crafted your agreements, commit them to paper. You could write
   them in a special journal, type them up and print them out, or even create
   an artistic representation. Some couples hold a small ceremony to read their
   code aloud to each other, adding a sense of significance and celebration to the
   moment.

7. **Revisit and Revise**

   Your Couple's Code is a living document. Make a plan to revisit it regularly—on
   your anniversary, at the start of a new year, or any time you feel it's needed.
   Celebrate your progress and adjust where necessary to reflect your evolving
   relationship.

• • • • ● • ● ● • • •

Common Challenges and How to Overcome Them

Creating a Couple's Code can be a rewarding process, but it's not always easy. Here are
some common challenges and ways to navigate them:

- **Differing values or needs**: What if you and your partner seem to want different
  things? Perhaps one of you craves more independence while the other longs for
  more togetherness. The key here is to get curious, not furious. Approach your
  differences with a spirit of empathy and creativity. Often, there's a way to honor

both partners' needs with a little flexibility and innovation. For example, if one partner needs more alone time, you could agree to designate certain evenings as "solo time" where you pursue separate activities, but then come back together for a nightly check-in or cuddle.

- **Struggling to follow through**: It's one thing to write down your agreements, but another to actually live them out. What if you find yourselves slipping back into old patterns or neglecting your commitments? First, extend yourselves some grace. Change is hard, and slipups are normal. When you notice yourself veering off course, simply name it without shame and recommit to your intentions. It can also help to build in regular accountability check-ins, where you reflect on how you're doing with your agreements and troubleshoot any obstacles. You might even consider involving a neutral third party, like a couples therapist, to support you in staying on track.

- **Feeling constrained or bored**: For some couples, the idea of a "rulebook" for their relationship feels stifling or unromantic. They worry that codifying their connection will sap the spontaneity and spark. If this resonates, try reframing your Couple's Code as a springboard, not a straitjacket. Your agreements are there to create a foundation of security and clarity, one that actually frees you up to be more playful and adventurous together. Think of your code like a dance floor—it provides a sturdy, reliable base, but how you dance upon it is up to you. In fact, you might even include some agreements specifically around trying new things or surprising each other to keep that sense of excitement alive.

· · · · ● · ● · · ·

Real-Life Codes: Stories of Couples Who Created Their Own Rulebook

Priya and David came from different cultural backgrounds and often struggled with navigating family expectations. Their Couple's Code included agreements like:

- "We will learn about and honor each other's cultural traditions, while also creating our own unique blend."

- "We will communicate openly about the pressures or expectations we feel from family, and always put our partnership first."

- "We will approach cultural differences with curiosity and respect, not judgment or stereotyping."

For *Adam and Isabel*, demanding careers left them feeling like ships passing in the night. Their Couple's Code focused on reclaiming connection amid their busy schedules, including commitments like:

- "We will have a nonnegotiable weekly date night, and take turns planning special activities."

- "We will not check work emails or take work calls during dinner or weekends."

- "We will take at least one 'unplugged' vacation together each year, where we leave our laptops behind."

- "We will support and celebrate each other's career successes, while also reminding each other that our relationship is the top priority."

· · · ● · ● · ● · ● · ● · ·

Building a Love That Lasts

Creating a Couple's Code is about being intentional in love. It's a practice of continually turning toward each other with curiosity, compassion, and commitment. Your code doesn't have to look like anyone else's—what matters is that it feels true and nourishing for your relationship.

Approach the process with a spirit of playfulness and possibility. Every agreement, every shared reflection, is a step in writing your love story.

Workbook Exercise: Couple's Code Creation

Now it's your turn to create your own Couple's Code! Set aside some extended time with your partner to work through this exercise together.

Step 1: Clarify Your Values

To begin, take some individual reflection time to consider your personal values. What principles guide your life? What qualities do you aspire to embody in your relationships?

Here are some questions to consider:

- What are the top 5 values you try to live by?

- What qualities do you most admire in others?

- What values do you want to be the foundation of your relationship?

After individual reflection, come together with your partner to share your reflections. Look for areas of overlap or complementarity in your values. Identify 3-5 core values you want your relationship to embody.

Step 2: Share Your Needs and Expectations

Next, take turns sharing your needs, desires, and expectations in each area of your relationship. Consider areas like:

- Communication and conflict resolution

- Intimacy and physical affection

- Quality time and shared activities

- Individual time and space

- Roles and responsibilities

- Finances and decision-making

- Family and community

As you share, practice deep listening. Seek to understand your partner's perspective, even if it differs from your own.

After sharing, reflect together:

- Where are your needs and expectations aligned?

- Where do you have differences to navigate?

- Where might you need to compromise or find creative solutions?

Step 3: Craft Your Agreements

Now, it's time to turn your shared understandings into concrete agreements. For each area of your relationship, work together to create specific, actionable commitments.

For example:

- "We agree to have a weekly 'State of the Union' check-in every Sunday evening to share appreciations, air any concerns, and align on plans for the week ahead."

- "We agree to prioritize intimacy by setting aside tech-free time together each night before bed, even if just for 15 minutes."

- "We agree to divide household chores evenly, with a rotating schedule that we revisit monthly."

As you craft your agreements, ensure they are:

- Specific and actionable

- Mutually agreed upon

- Realistic and achievable

- Reflective of both partners' needs

Step 4: Make it Official

Once you've drafted your agreements, it's time to make your Couple's Code official!

Choose a format that feels meaningful to you. You could:

- Write your code in a special journal

- Create an artistic representation to hang in your home

- Have a ceremony to read your code aloud to each other

- Sign and frame your written code

- Create a digital document you both have access to

The key is to give your code a sense of significance and permanence. This is your relationship's charter, the constitution of your love.

Step 5: Live It and Revisit It

Creating your Couple's Code is just the beginning. The real work is in living it day to day.

Make a plan for how you'll incorporate your agreements into your daily life. You might:

- Read your code together regularly as a reminder

- Schedule regular check-ins to reflect on how you're doing

- Create visual reminders of your key agreements

- Celebrate successes and recalibrate after missteps

Remember, your Couple's Code is a living document. As you grow and your relationship evolves, revisit and update your code to reflect your current realities and aspirations.

Creating a Couple's Code is an act of love, trust, and intentionality. By taking this step, you're investing in the long-term health and happiness of your relationship. So dive in with open hearts and minds. Embrace the process of discovering and articulating what matters most to you as a couple.

---

1. Matthews, 2015

Part II: Who Am I? Know Your Boundaries to Love Better

CHAPTER THREE

YOUR PERSONAL BOUNDARY BLUEPRINT: WHO ARE YOU AND WHAT DO YOU NEED?

Before you can begin building healthy boundaries in your relationship, there's a crucial first step: understanding yourself. Knowing your own needs, desires, and limits is the foundation upon which all boundaries are built.

Think of it like building a house. You wouldn't just start throwing up walls at random—you'd begin with a blueprint, a clear, detailed plan of what you want to create and how you want it to function. In the same way, your personal boundary blueprint is a roadmap of your inner landscape—your values, vulnerabilities, deal-breakers, and dreams. When you're clear about what matters to you, you can start constructing external boundaries that support and protect your well-being.

• • • **•** • **•** • **•** • •

The Power of Self-Knowledge

Self-awareness isn't just a nice-to-have—it's a relationship necessity. Research shows that self-awareness is linked to greater relationship satisfaction, improved communication, and healthier conflict resolution[1].

When you know yourself, you show up in your partnership with more authenticity and confidence. You communicate your needs clearly, make choices that align with your values, and create space for deeper connection.

Without self-knowledge, you're more likely to let others cross your boundaries, project your unresolved emotions onto your partner, or get stuck in reactive cycles. Doing the inner work of self-discovery isn't indulgence—it's preparation for building a strong and fulfilling relationship.

For *Emma,* this lesson became clear when she realized she was constantly feeling resentful and overwhelmed in her marriage. She often said yes to things she didn't want to do, feeling that she had to compromise to keep the peace. In therapy, Emma discovered that she struggled to recognize and honor her own limits. Growing up, she'd learned to equate having needs with selfishness, which made setting boundaries feel nearly impossible.

As Emma explored her own needs and desires, she began to uncover an inner world she had long ignored. She found that she loved quiet evenings at home, despite always agreeing to social plans. She realized she needed more downtime to recharge. Armed with this self-knowledge, she started setting boundaries that respected her needs—saying no to draining invitations and asking for solitude when she needed it. This not only improved her own well-being but strengthened her marriage. By showing up as her authentic self, Emma invited her husband to do the same.

• • • ● • ● • • •

The Neuroscience of Self-Knowledge

Self-awareness doesn't just have psychological benefits—it has neurological ones as well. When you engage in self-reflection, you're actually rewiring your brain. Studies show that self-reflection activates the brain's default mode network, which is responsible for autobiographical memory, self-referential thinking, and imagining the future[2].

In other words, when we turn our attention inward and explore our inner worlds, we're strengthening the neural pathways that allow us to make sense of our experiences, learn from the past, and envision new possibilities for ourselves.

This rewiring strengthens the neural pathways that help you make sense of your experiences, learn from the past, and envision new possibilities. When you know yourself, you communicate more effectively, avoid unhealthy codependency, and build relationships that nourish you on a deeper level.

This has profound implications for our relationships. When we have a clearer sense of who we are and what we need, we're better able to communicate those needs to our partners. We're less likely to fall into codependent patterns of self-abandonment or resentment. We're more likely to attract and sustain relationships that truly nourish and support us.

Moreover, self-knowledge is a key component of emotional intelligence, which research links to relationship success. When you understand your own emotional triggers and reactions, you're better equipped to respond constructively in your relationships.

Boundaries and the Brain

What does all this have to do with boundaries? Quite a lot. Setting and maintaining boundaries trains your brain to feel safer and more secure. Boundaries signal to your nervous system that you're in control of your well-being, which reduces the stress response and helps you feel calmer.

Think about it this way: When someone crosses your boundaries—whether it's a partner who consistently shows up late, a friend who gossips about you, or a coworker who dumps their work on you—your brain registers this as a threat. Your amygdala, the brain's "alarm system," gets activated, triggering a cascade of stress hormones like cortisol and adrenaline[3].

Over time, chronic boundary violations can keep your nervous system stuck in this hypervigilant, reactive state. You might find yourself feeling anxious, resentful, or exhausted, without fully knowing why.

On the other hand, when you set and enforce clear boundaries, your brain learns that it can relax and let its guard down. You begin to associate boundary-setting with feelings of safety, empowerment, and control. This makes it easier to show up as a calm, present, and engaged partner.

This has cascading effects on your overall well-being and your relationships. When you're not constantly in fight-or-flight mode, you have more mental and emotional bandwidth to be present, engaged, and empathetic with your loved ones. You're able to respond rather than react, to communicate rather than defend.

Moreover, setting boundaries is an act of self-respect and self-love. It's a way of honoring your own inherent worth and dignity. And when you treat yourself with respect, you naturally invite others to do the same.

Setting boundaries is also an act of self-respect. By honoring your needs, you create space for others to respect you too. As Brené Brown writes, *"Daring to set boundaries is about having the courage to love ourselves, even when we risk disappointing others"*[4].

• • • • • • • • • •

Elements of Your Boundary Blueprint

So, what goes into your personal boundary blueprint? Here are the key elements:

- **Values**: What principles and qualities are most important to you? What do you want to stand for in your life and relationship? Examples might include honesty, autonomy, growth, or contribution.

- **Needs**: What do you need to feel safe, respected, and fulfilled? This could include physical needs like rest and nutrition, emotional needs like affection and reassurance, or spiritual needs like meaning and purpose. Remember, needs are non-negotiable—they're the bare minimum of what you require to thrive.

- **Desires**: What do you truly want? What lights you up and brings you joy? Don't censor yourself—give yourself permission to name your deepest longings. Desires might encompass things like adventure, creativity, sensuality, or self-expression.

- **Limits**: What are your non-negotiables? What lines do you need to draw to protect your well-being? This could include things like "I won't tolerate dishonesty," "I need at least an hour to myself each day," or "I don't work on weekends."

- **Fears and vulnerabilities**: What makes you feel exposed or threatened? What past hurts or traumas still impact you? Naming these tender spots can help you understand where you might need extra protection or support. For example, if you have a history of being taken advantage of financially, you might have a heightened need for transparency and equity in your joint finances.

- **Strengths and gifts**: What unique qualities and abilities do you bring to the table? What makes you feel empowered and confident? Owning your strengths can help you set boundaries from a place of self-worth. If you know you're a skilled communicator, for instance, you can lean on that strength to express your needs clearly and compassionately.

Remember, your boundary blueprint is a living document. As you grow and change, your needs and desires will evolve too. Stay curious about your inner world and adapt your boundaries as needed.

• • • ● • ● • ● • • •

Real-Life Examples of Boundary Blueprints

Isabella's Story: Isabella had always struggled to assert her needs in her relationship, often going along with whatever her partner wanted to avoid conflict. But after reflecting on her boundary blueprint, Isabella realized that her fear of rejection was keeping her from speaking up. With this new awareness, she started small—asking her partner for a night off from cooking or a few quiet hours to herself. Each time she successfully asserted a boundary, her confidence grew. Eventually, Isabella learned to set boundaries around bigger needs, like career choices and personal time, and her relationship transformed into one where her voice was heard and valued.

Linh and Tom's Journey: Linh and Tom came to couples therapy because they kept having the same fight over and over. Linh wanted more quality time together, while Tom wanted more space to pursue his hobbies. In exploring their boundary blueprints, Linh and Tom uncovered some key differences in their needs and expectations. Linh's primary love language was quality time—she felt most cared for when she and Tom were engaging in shared activities and deep conversations. Tom, on the other hand, was more of an acts of service person—he showed his love by taking care of practical tasks and giving Linh space to recharge. As they dug deeper, they also discovered some underlying fears and vulnerabilities. Linh had a deep-seated fear of abandonment stemming from her father leaving when she was young. When Tom wanted more independence, she subconsciously interpreted it as a sign that he was pulling away from her. Tom, meanwhile, had grown up in a household where his personal boundaries were constantly invaded. His mother would barge into his room without knocking, read his diary, and interrogate him about his friendships. As a result, he had an intense need for privacy and autonomy. Armed with this new understanding, Linh and Tom were able to approach their differences with more empathy and creativity. Instead of seeing each other's needs as a threat, they started to view them as an opportunity for growth. They agreed to set aside certain evenings for dedicated couple time, where they would focus solely on connecting with each other. On other nights, they gave each other permission to do their own thing, trusting that this individual time would actually fuel their relationship. They also developed a ritual around transitions and reunions. When Tom needed alone time, he would give Linh a long hug and express his excitement to reconnect with her later. When he returned, they would take a few minutes to share highlights from their time apart. This helped Linh feel secure and valued, even in the midst of distance. By honoring each other's boundary blueprints, Linh and Tom were able to turn their recurring conflict into an opportunity for deeper understanding and intimacy. They learned to love each other not in spite of their differences, but because of them.

• • • ● • ● • ● • •

Overcoming Obstacles to Self-Knowledge

The path to self-knowledge and boundary-setting can be challenging. Many of us face internal and external obstacles, including:

- **Childhood conditioning**: Many of us were taught to prioritize others' needs over our own, making it difficult to honor our boundaries.

- **Trauma**: Past experiences of abuse or neglect can make it hard to trust our needs or feel safe asserting them.

- **Fear of rejection**: Boundaries often require us to risk others' disapproval, which can feel threatening to our sense of belonging.

- **Societal pressures**: Gender roles, cultural expectations, and marginalization can add extra layers of complexity to boundary-setting.

While these challenges are real, they're not insurmountable. Therapy, self-reflection, supportive relationships, and advocacy can all help you reclaim your right to set boundaries.

Crafting Your Personal Blueprint

Ready to start crafting your personal boundary blueprint? Here's how to begin:

1. **Create a Sacred Space**

   Find a quiet, comfortable place where you can reflect without interruptions. Light a candle or play soothing music to create a calming atmosphere.

2. **Reflect on Your Blueprint Elements**

   Jot down your thoughts on the key elements of your boundary blueprint: values, needs, desires, limits, fears, and strengths. Let your truth flow freely without censoring yourself.

3. **Look for patterns and themes:**

   Once you've done a brain dump, look back over your reflections. What themes or throughlines do you notice? Are there certain needs or values that come up again and again? Circle or highlight anything that feels particularly resonant.

4. **Identify Your Non-Negotiables**

   Review your reflections and identify the boundaries that feel essential to your well-being. These are your non-negotiables—the limits that must be respected for you to feel safe and fulfilled.

5. **Refine and organize:**

   Synthesize your reflections into a clear, concise document. You might organize it by category, or distill it down to a few key bullet points. The format is less important than the clarity and conviction behind it. One helpful framework is to create a "needs/wants/dealbreakers" list. For each category, aim to identify 3-5 key items. For example:

- **Needs (non-negotiable, must-haves)**

Daily affection and physical touch

Regular quality time and focused attention

Honesty and transparency

Respect for my need for alone time

6. **Share with Your Partner**

   Once you've crafted your blueprint, share it with your partner. Approach the conversation with openness and curiosity, inviting them to share their own reflections.

Final Reflections

Boundaries are an act of self-love. By setting and honoring them, you're creating a foundation for deeper connection, trust, and intimacy. Your boundary blueprint is your guide to living and loving with integrity—let it light the way.

Workbook Exercise: Boundary Blueprint Worksheet

Creating a personal boundary blueprint is a powerful act of self-discovery and self-care. This worksheet will guide you through the process of exploring your values, needs, fears, and dealbreakers to craft a clear vision of what you require to feel safe, respected, and fulfilled in relationships.

Before you begin, create a safe and sacred space for this important inner work. Find a quiet, comfortable spot where you won't be interrupted. You might light a candle, make a cup of tea, or put on some soothing music to signal to yourself that this is a time for deep reflection and self-honoring.

Gather your materials: a journal or notebook, some pens or pencils, and any other supplies that support your creative process (art supplies, collaging materials, etc.). Give yourself permission to let your thoughts and feelings flow freely, without judgment or censorship.

Part 1: Excavating Your Truth

In this first section, you'll do a deep dive into your inner world, exploring the various elements that make up your unique boundary blueprint. For each prompt, take your time and write down whatever comes to mind. Don't worry about editing or making sense of it yet—the goal is simply to get your truth onto the page.

1. **Values**

   ○ What principles or qualities are most important to you in life and relationships?

   ○ When you imagine your ideal self, what values are you embodying?

- What values did your family of origin prioritize? How have those influenced your own values?

- Reflect on a time when you felt your values were honored in a relationship. What did that feel like?

- Reflect on a time when you felt your values were compromised in a relationship. What did that feel like?

2. **Needs**

- What do you need to feel safe, respected, and cared for in a relationship?

- What do you need to feel emotionally secure and connected?

- What do you need to feel physically comfortable and well?

- What do you need to feel intellectually stimulated and engaged?

- What do you need to feel spiritually nourished and aligned?

- Think about your various roles and identities (e.g., partner, parent, employee, friend, artist, etc.). What unique needs arise in each domain?

3. **Desires**

- What do you deeply long for in relationships and in life?

- What lights you up and brings you joy?

- What experiences or qualities do you wish you had more of?

- If you could wave a magic wand and have your ideal relationship(s), what would they look and feel like?

- What adventures or experiences do you yearn to have?

- What secret dreams or fantasies do you hold close to your heart?

4. **Fears**

- What are you most afraid of in relationships?

- What past hurts or traumas still impact you today?

- What situations or dynamics tend to trigger feelings of anxiety, insecurity, or defensiveness for you?

- What parts of yourself do you tend to hide or minimize out of fear of rejection?

- What catastrophes or worst-case scenarios do you secretly worry about?

- How do you typically cope with or avoid your fears?

5. **Dealbreakers**

- What behaviors or situations would signal the end of a relationship for you?

- What are your absolute no-gos, under any circumstances?

- What compromises or sacrifices are you unwilling to make, even for love?

- What qualities or dynamics feel intolerable or unacceptable to you?

- What boundaries, if crossed, would irrevocably break your trust?

- What personal values, goals, or needs are you unwilling to give up?

Take a break if you need to. This is deep, tender work. Stretch, breathe, and give yourself some love and compassion for showing up so bravely and honestly.

Part 2: Identifying Patterns and Priorities

In this next section, you'll review your free-writes from Part 1 and start to identify key themes, patterns, and priorities. The goal is to distill your reflections into a clearer, more focused boundary blueprint.

1. **Review your writing**:

- Read back through your free-writes slowly and attentively.

- Highlight or underline any words, phrases, or themes that jump out at you as particularly important or resonant.

- Notice any patterns or recurring ideas that emerge across different categories.

2. **Identify your core values**:

- Based on your values free-write and your review, choose 3-5 core values that feel most essential and non-negotiable to you.

- Write these core values at the top of a new page.

3. **Identify your key needs**:

- Review your needs free-write and your highlights.

- Choose 5-7 needs that feel most crucial for your well-being and fulfillment in relationships.

- Write these key needs under your core values.

4. **Identify your deepest desires**:

- Review your desires free-write and your highlights.

- Choose 3-5 desires that feel most alive and exciting to you.

- Write these deepest desires under your key needs.

5. **Identify your biggest fears**:

- Review your fears free-write and your highlights.

- Choose 3-5 fears that feel most potent or impactful for you.

- Write these biggest fears under your deepest desires.

6. **Identify your dealbreakers**:

- Review your dealbreakers free-write and your highlights.

- Choose 3-5 dealbreakers that feel most clear and non-negotiable for you.

- Write these dealbreakers at the bottom of your page.

Take a step back and look at your page. You should now have a focused list of your core values, key needs, deepest desires, biggest fears, and bottom-line dealbreakers. This is the skeleton of your personal boundary blueprint.

Part 3: Crafting Your Blueprint

In this final section, you'll flesh out your blueprint skeleton into a clear, actionable guide for setting and maintaining healthy boundaries in your relationships.

1. **Write a boundary statement for each core value**:

- Look at your first core value. What boundary do you need to set to honor and protect this value?

- Write a clear, specific boundary statement. For example, if one of your core values is honesty, your boundary statement might be: "I need my partner to tell me the truth, even when it's difficult. Lying or withholding important information is not acceptable to me."

- Repeat this process for each of your core values.

2. **Write a request for each key need**:

- Look at your first key need. What do you need from your partner(s) or from yourself to meet this need?

- Write a clear, specific request. For example, if one of your key needs is quality time, your request might be: "I need at least one uninterrupted hour of one-on-one time with my partner each day to feel connected and cared for."

- Repeat this process for each of your key needs.

3. **Write an aspiration for each deepest desire**:

- Look at your first deepest desire. What would it look and feel like to fully honor and express this desire? What boundaries might you need to set to create space for this desire?

- Write a vivid, inspiring aspiration. For example, if one of your deepest desires is adventure, your aspiration might be: "I give myself full permission to regularly seek out new experiences and adventures, both on my own and with my partner. I communicate my plans and desires openly, and trust that my independence and curiosity will be celebrated."

- Repeat this process for each of your deepest desires.

4. **Write a safety plan for each biggest fear**:

- Look at your first biggest fear. What boundaries, support systems, or coping strategies do you need to feel safe and secure in the face of this fear?

- Write a detailed safety plan. For example, if one of your biggest fears is abandonment, your safety plan might include: "If I'm feeling insecure or afraid in my relationship, I will: 1) Name my fear out loud to my partner and ask for reassurance. 2) Reach out to my support system for validation and compassion. 3) Remind myself that I am inherently worthy and lovable, regardless of my relationship status."

- Repeat this process for each of your biggest fears.

5. **Write a bottom line for each dealbreaker**:

- Look at your first dealbreaker. What consequence or action will you take if this boundary is violated?

- Write a clear, firm bottom line. For example, if one of your dealbreakers is physical violence, your bottom line might be: "If my partner ever hits me or uses any form of physical force against me, I will leave the relationship immediately and seek safety and support."

     ○ Repeat this process for each of your dealbreakers.

6. **Organize and refine your blueprint**:

     ○ Type or rewrite your boundary statements, requests, aspirations, safety plans, and bottom lines into a clear, organized document.

     ○ Review your blueprint for clarity and specificity. Make any necessary edits or adjustments.

     ○ Consider adding a brief introduction or conclusion that summarizes your overall approach to boundaries and self-care in relationships.

Congratulations! You now have a comprehensive personal boundary blueprint. Take some time to read through it, feeling the power and clarity of your own truth. Consider sharing your blueprint with trusted loved ones, including your partner(s). Remember, healthy boundaries are a gift to your relationships—they create the safety and trust necessary for real intimacy and connection.

Keep your blueprint somewhere easily accessible. Commit to reviewing it regularly, especially when faced with difficult decisions or relationship challenges. Allow it to be a living document, one that grows and evolves along with you.

Above all, let your blueprint be a daily reminder of your inherent worthiness, your fundamental right to safety and respect, and your amazing capacity for self-love and self-advocacy. You've done profound and courageous work today. May it serve you well on your ongoing journey to healthier, happier, more fulfilling relationships.

---

1. Sutton, 2016

2. Molnar-Szakacs & Uddin, 2013

3. Rodrigues, LeDoux, & Sapolsky, 2009

4. Brown, 2010

CHAPTER FOUR

THE BOUNDARIES WHISPERER: ASSERT WITHOUT THE AWKWARDNESS

You've done the inner work of excavating your personal boundary blueprint. You're clear on your values, needs, desires, fears, and dealbreakers. Now comes the next step: communicating those boundaries to others. This is where many of us stumble.

We often worry that setting boundaries will make us seem demanding or unkind. There's a fear of rejection or abandonment if we speak our truth. We may get tongue-tied when someone crosses a boundary or find ourselves avoiding the conversation altogether.

But here's the truth: asserting boundaries doesn't have to be confrontational. When done with clarity and compassion, boundary-setting can deepen intimacy and trust. It allows you to show up authentically and honor your needs while also respecting the needs of others.

In this chapter, we'll explore the art of asserting boundaries skillfully and compassionately. You'll learn practical tools for clear, calm communication, strategies for handling boundary challenges, and how to view boundary-setting as an act of self-love and relational care.

• • • • ● • ● • ● • • •

Why Asserting Boundaries Can Feel Hard

Before diving into the "how-to," let's acknowledge why boundary-setting can feel so difficult. Some common fears include:

- **Fear of rejection or abandonment:** We worry that asserting boundaries will make us seem "too much" or "too difficult," and that loved ones will pull away.

- **Guilt or self-doubt:** We question whether our needs are valid, feeling guilty for taking up space.

- **Conflict avoidance:** For those who grew up in households where conflict was unsafe, any confrontation may feel terrifying.

- **Lack of models or skills:** Many of us didn't see healthy boundary-setting growing up, so we're navigating uncharted territory.

- **People-pleasing tendencies:** If we've always prioritized others, asserting our needs can feel uncomfortable and foreign.

These fears are understandable, but they don't have to keep you stuck. With practice and support, you can learn to assert your boundaries confidently and kindly. Boundary-setting is not selfish—it's a cornerstone of healthy, sustainable relationships.

• • • ● • ● • ● • • •

The Three Keys to Asserting Boundaries

From my work with individuals and couples, I've identified three key principles that underlie effective boundary assertion:

1. **Clarity**: Be crystal clear about what your boundary is and why it matters to you. When you know exactly what you need, you can communicate it clearly and confidently.

2. **Compassion**: Approach boundary-setting from a place of care and respect, both for yourself and for the other person. Boundaries aren't about control; they're about creating safety and trust.

3. **Consistency**: Reinforce your boundaries consistently over time. Mixed messages or frequent exceptions undermine your limits and invite confusion or pushback.

Let's explore each of these principles in more depth.

1. Clarity

The first step in asserting a boundary is clarity—knowing exactly what you need and why. Without this clarity, you might struggle to communicate your limits effectively.

Take *Sophia*, for example. She was frustrated in her relationship with her live-in partner, Jamie. "I just need more space," she said. But "more space" was too vague. She worked to identify specific boundaries that she needed:

- Having two nights a week to herself without the expectation of socializing with Jamie.

- Keeping her art studio as a private space, free from interruptions.

- Going to bed and waking up on her own schedule, even if it differed from Jamie's.

With this clarity, Sophia could communicate her needs in a clear and actionable way:

- "Jamie, I need Tuesday and Thursday evenings to myself to recharge. Can you make plans with friends or do something solo on those nights?"

- "When I'm working in my studio, I need complete focus and solitude. Please don't come in or interrupt me unless it's an emergency. If you need something, could you send me a text and I'll get back to you when I'm at a stopping point?"

- "I know our sleep schedules are different, and that's okay. I need to honor my own natural rhythms to feel rested and healthy. Let's figure out a way to go to bed and wake up separately without disturbing each other."

Notice how these boundaries are specific and actionable. When you're clear about your limits, it's easier to communicate them in a grounded, reasonable way.

Questions to help you clarify your boundaries:

- What behaviors or situations feel uncomfortable or unsafe to me?

- What do I need more or less of in this relationship to feel respected and cared for?

- How will honoring this boundary improve my well-being and the relationship?

- What specific requests can I make to ensure my boundary is respected?

2. Compassion

Once you're clear on your boundary, the next step is communicating it to others with compassion. This means approaching the conversation from a place of care and respect, both for yourself and for the other person.

It's easy to fall into the trap of seeing boundaries as a way to control or punish others. We might use them to lash out in anger, or to make demands without considering the impact on the other person.

But true boundary-setting is not about attacking or blaming. It's about taking responsibility for your own needs and limits, while also extending understanding and empathy to the other person's perspective.

This compassionate approach is rooted in the work of Marshall Rosenberg, the founder of Nonviolent Communication (NVC). Rosenberg teaches that all human beings have basic needs for safety, connection, and understanding. When we can communicate our boundaries in a way that acknowledges and validates these universal needs, we invite cooperation and care rather than defensiveness and conflict.

Here's a simple NVC formula for expressing a boundary with compassion:

"When [describe the behavior or situation that crosses your boundary], I feel [name your emotions]. I need [state your boundary clearly]. Would you be willing to [make a specific request]?"

Let's see how this might play out in a real-life example:

Anita had been dating Marco for a few months when she started to feel smothered by his constant texting. He would message her throughout the day, expecting immediate responses, and get upset when she was slow to reply.

At first, Anita ignored her discomfort, not wanting to hurt Marco's feelings. But as the pattern continued, she realized she needed to set a clear boundary around communication.

She invited Marco out for coffee and shared the following:

"When I receive texts from you throughout the workday, I feel anxious and pressured to respond right away. I need to be able to focus on my job during work hours without distractions or interruptions. Would you be willing to limit your texts to urgent matters only between 9am and 5pm, and wait for me to respond when I'm available in the evenings?"

Notice how Anita's boundary statement follows the NVC formula:

- She clearly describes the behavior that's crossing her boundary (constant texting throughout the workday)

- She names her emotions (anxiety, pressure)

- She states her need (focus on work without interruptions)

- She makes a specific, actionable request (limit non-urgent texts during work hours)

By expressing her boundary in this way, Anita invites Marco to understand her perspective and needs. She's not attacking him as a person or making him wrong for his behavior. She's simply taking responsibility for her own limits and making a clear request for how they can be respected.

Of course, even the most compassionate boundary-setting can be met with resistance or pushback. The other person might feel hurt, angry, or defensive. They might try to argue or negotiate with your limit.

This is where your own self-compassion and emotional resilience come in. It's important to remember that you're not responsible for the other person's reactions or emotions. You're only responsible for expressing your truth as kindly and clearly as you can.

If you encounter resistance, you can acknowledge the other person's feelings while still holding firm to your boundary:

"I understand this is difficult to hear, and it makes sense that you're feeling frustrated. At the same time, this is what I need to feel safe and respected in our relationship. I hope we can find a way to honor both of our needs moving forward."

You might need to repeat your boundary multiple times, or even take some space from the conversation if it becomes unproductive. But by approaching the interaction with compassion for both yourself and the other person, you create the conditions for genuine understanding and collaboration.

Compassionate boundary-setting is a practice, not a perfect destination. There will be times when you slip up, when you express your limits clumsily or reactively. That's okay. What matters is your commitment to self-honesty and relational care, your willingness to keep showing up with an open heart.

3. Consistency

Finally, consistency is crucial to effective boundary-setting. Boundaries require ongoing reinforcement—especially when life gets messy, and people test the limits.

Consider your boundaries like a garden that needs regular attention. If someone repeatedly crosses a boundary—say, showing up late after agreeing to be punctual—you need to address the issue directly rather than brushing it off.

For example:
"Hey, I've noticed you've been late to our plans a lot lately. I know things come up, but it feels disrespectful of my time. Can we talk about how to handle changes in the future?"

Consistency means calmly reaffirming your boundaries, even when it's uncomfortable. It's easy to let boundaries slide when someone pushes back, but that undermines your limits and creates confusion.

Upholding your boundaries sends the message that you value yourself and expect others to do the same. While it may feel uncomfortable at times, consistency strengthens your sense of self-trust and signals to others that your boundaries are non-negotiable.

Putting It All Together

To summarize, asserting boundaries with clarity, compassion, and consistency allows you to navigate relationships with confidence and respect. While it may feel daunting at first, practicing these skills will deepen your capacity for authentic connection and self-love.

Boundary-setting is a lifelong practice, not a one-time event. You'll have moments of doubt and discomfort, but each step builds your confidence. Over time, you'll see the benefits: healthier relationships, more personal freedom, and greater peace of mind.

Workbook Exercise: Boundary Assertion Scripts

Now that you understand the three keys to asserting boundaries with clarity, compassion, and consistency, it's time to put these principles into practice. In this exercise, you'll have the opportunity to craft and refine your own boundary assertion scripts for common challenging situations.

Remember, the goal is not to memorize and recite these scripts robotically. Rather, it's to develop your muscle for expressing your needs and limits in a way that feels grounded, respectful, and authentic to you. Think of these scripts as training wheels—a supportive structure to help you build confidence and skill over time.

Instructions

1. **Choose your scenarios**: Below, you'll find a list of common boundary-challenging situations. Choose 3-5 scenarios that feel most relevant or challenging for you currently. Feel free to adapt the specifics to fit your own life circumstances.

2. **Craft your script**: For each scenario you chose, write out a brief script for how you might assert your boundary in that situation. Try to include the following elements:

   ○ A clear description of the behavior or situation that's crossing your boundary

   ○ An "I statement" expressing your feelings and needs

   ○ A specific request for how you'd like your boundary to be respected going forward

   ○ A compassionate acknowledgement of the other person's perspective or feelings

3. Here's a template you can use: "When [describe boundary-crossing behavior], I feel [your feelings]. I need [your boundary]. Would you be willing to [specific request]? I understand [compassionate acknowledgement]."

4. **Refine and practice**: Read over your scripts and make any edits or refinements to make them feel more clear, concise, or authentic to your voice. Then, practice saying them out loud to yourself in the mirror or to a trusted friend or support person. Notice how it feels in your body to give voice to your boundaries. Acknowledge any discomfort or resistance that arises, and meet it with compassion.

5. **Reflect and integrate**: After practicing your scripts, take a few minutes to

reflect on the experience. What felt easy or natural? What felt challenging or awkward? What do you want to remember or work on as you continue to build your boundary-setting skills? Write down any insights or intentions.

Boundary Scenario Prompts

Feel free to choose from these common scenarios, or create your own based on your current life situation:

1. A friend consistently shows up late or cancels plans at the last minute.

2. Your partner makes a major purchase or financial decision without consulting you.

3. A family member critiques or questions your personal choices (e.g., your career, your parenting style, your appearance).

4. A coworker frequently interrupts you or takes credit for your ideas in meetings.

5. Your in-laws drop by unannounced or overstay their welcome in your home.

6. Your partner discloses private information about you to others without your consent.

7. A friend or family member pressures you to drink alcohol or use substances when you've expressed a desire not to.

8. A romantic interest continues to pursue you or send flirtatious messages after you've communicated your lack of interest.

9. A colleague or client contacts you excessively outside of work hours or expects immediate responses to non-urgent matters.

10. A neighbor plays loud music late at night, disrupting your sleep or peace.

Remember, these are just prompts to get you started. The most important thing is to choose scenarios that feel relevant and meaningful to your own life and relationships.

Sample Scripts

Here are a few examples of what your boundary assertion scripts might look like:

1. **Scenario**: A friend consistently shows up late or cancels plans at the last minute. **Script**: "When you cancel our plans at the last minute, I feel frustrated and disrespected. I need to be able to count on our scheduled time together. Would you be willing to give me at least 24 hours' notice if you need to cancel or reschedule? I understand that emergencies come up, and I'm happy to be flexible when needed. I value our friendship and want to find a way to make plans that works for both of us."

2. **Scenario**: Your partner makes a major purchase or financial decision without consulting you. **Script**: "When you made that large purchase without talking to me first, I felt surprised and left out of the decision-making process. I need financial transparency and collaboration in our relationship. Would you be willing to commit to discussing any expenses over [$ amount] together before moving forward? I understand you may have had good intentions or felt pressure to act quickly. I care about building a partnership where we make important choices as a team."

3. **Scenario**: A family member critiques or questions your personal choices. **Script**: "When you criticize my [career/parenting/lifestyle] choices, I feel judged and unsupported. I need you to respect that these are my decisions to make, even if you disagree with them. Would you be willing to express any concerns you have directly and respectfully, and then trust me to navigate my own path? I understand you may be coming from a place of love or concern. I value our relationship and appreciate your support, even when we see things differently."

Remember, these are just examples. The most effective scripts will be the ones that feel authentic and resonant to you and your specific situation.

Reflection Prompts

After practicing your boundary assertion scripts, take a few minutes to reflect on the experience. Here are some prompts to guide your reflection:

1. What felt empowering or liberating about expressing my boundaries in this way? What fears or doubts did I notice coming up?

2. How did it feel in my body to speak my truth and assert my needs? What sensations or emotions arose?

3. What inner resources (e.g., self-compassion, courage, clarity) did I draw upon to support me in this practice? What additional support or resources could help me feel more skilled and confident in boundary-setting?

4. What do I want to remember or take forward as I continue to practice asserting my boundaries in real-life situations?

5. How might consistently honoring my boundaries impact my relationship with myself and others over time? What hopes or intentions do I have for this ongoing growth edge?

Remember, boundary-setting is a lifelong practice, not a one-time event. Be patient and compassionate with yourself as you learn and grow. Celebrate each small step you take to honor your needs and limits.

And know that every time you assert a boundary, you're not just standing up for yourself—you're contributing to a world where all people feel empowered to live and love with authenticity, dignity, and care.

Part III: The Rules of Engagement: Boundaries in Action

CHAPTER FIVE

THE COMMUNICATION WALTZ: BOUNDARIES AND TALKING IT OUT WITHOUT THE DRAMA

Communication. The lifeblood of relationships. The key to intimacy. The foundation of all human connection. Easy, right? Well, not exactly. If you're like most people, you've likely faced communication breakdowns, misunderstandings, or full-on arguments over the smallest things—like whose turn it is to do the dishes, which somehow spirals into a heated debate about much bigger things.

But don't worry! In this chapter, we'll explore how to navigate the delicate dance of communication with your partner, all while keeping your boundaries intact and your sanity preserved. We'll learn how to express your needs, listen with empathy, and find win-win solutions, even in the face of conflict or strong emotions.

Think of it like a dance—a coordinated effort where both partners move in sync, even if you're just in sweatpants, eating leftover pizza, and talking through life's challenges.

• • • • • • • • • •

Why Communication Matters for Boundaries

Good communication is essential for healthy boundaries. Boundaries rely on the clear expression of your needs, limits, and expectations. Without effective communication, boundaries can blur, leaving you stewing in frustration rather than expressing what you need to feel safe and respected.

For instance, if your partner leaves their socks on the floor every day, you could silently seethe, or you could clearly express your need for a tidy space. Similarly, if your boundary around work-life balance is violated, it's easy to say yes to extra responsibilities because you don't know how to say no assertively. Either scenario can cause unnecessary tension.

On the flip side, communicating boundaries clearly and compassionately builds trust and respect. Your partner knows where you stand, and together you can navigate challenges more easily.

But let's be real: communication can be hard. It's vulnerable, it can be messy, and it often requires us to confront our fears of rejection, misunderstanding, or conflict. When emotions run high, breakdowns happen. But, like any skill, communication can be improved with practice. And with intention and compassion, you can master the art of boundary-supporting dialogue.

• • • ● • ● • • •

Common Communication Pitfalls (and How to Avoid Them)

Before diving into boundary-supporting communication strategies, let's look at some common pitfalls that trip people up. Do any of these sound familiar?

1. **Mind Reading**: Assuming you know what your partner is thinking or feeling without asking. For example, "I just KNOW they're mad at me because I forgot to take out the trash."

2. **Hint Dropping**: Expecting your partner to pick up on subtle cues instead of stating your needs directly. "I've been sighing loudly at the overflowing laundry hamper—why haven't they done anything?"

3. **Kitchen Sinking**: Bringing up past grievances during a present conflict. "Remember that time five years ago when you forgot our anniversary? I never got over that!"

4. **Blame and Criticism**: Attacking your partner instead of expressing your feelings. "You're so selfish—you never think about anyone but yourself."

5. **Defensiveness**: Counter-attacking or justifying your behavior instead of listening. "Well, if I'm selfish, what about all the times I've helped you with your work deadlines?"

We've all fallen into these traps, often driven by deeper fears like not being enough, fear of rejection, or losing control. These reactive patterns disconnect us from our partners and prevent meaningful dialogue.

But with practice, you can learn to recognize and avoid these pitfalls.

Here are a few tips:

- **Make the implicit explicit**: If you find yourself hinting or assuming, pause and ask, "What do I really need? How can I say that directly?"

- **Stay present**: When past hurts or future worries creep in, bring your focus back to the current issue. What is the core need right now?

- **Use "I" statements**: Rather than blaming, express your feelings and needs with "I" statements. "I feel hurt when we go days without quality time. I need more connection."

- **Listen to understand**: Resist the urge to defend yourself and instead focus on understanding your partner's perspective.

- **Take timeouts**: If a conversation escalates, take a break to cool off and revisit it later with a clearer mind.

These tips can help you move toward more loving, honest, and respectful communication.

• • • ● • ● • ● • ● • •

The Three C's of Boundary-Supporting Communication

Now that we've covered what NOT to do, let's focus on three key strategies for healthy communication: **Clarity, Compassion, and Curiosity**.

1. Clarity

The first key is clarity—being direct, specific, and honest about what you need, want, and feel. No hinting, hedging, or vagueness.

Clarity is an act of respect both for yourself and your partner. When you're clear about your boundaries, it frees you from resentment and gives your partner the opportunity to meet your needs.

Here are some tips for clarity:

- **Use direct, concise language**: Avoid vague or wishy-washy statements like "I don't know, what do you think?" or "It's fine, whatever you want." Instead, practice making clear, assertive statements like "I need some alone time this weekend to recharge" or "I'm not comfortable with you going through my phone without my permission."

- **Be specific about your needs and expectations**: Instead of saying "I wish you were more affectionate," try something like "I would love it if we could cuddle on the couch for at least 20 minutes every evening." The more specific you can be, the easier it is for your partner to understand and meet your needs.

- **Own your feelings and experiences**: Use "I" statements to express your own perspective, rather than making accusations or generalizations. "I feel anxious when you're out late without checking in" instead of "You never think about how your actions affect me!"

- **Be honest about your limits and dealbreakers**: Don't be afraid to communicate your hard lines and non-negotiables. "I'm not willing to have unprotected sex" or "I need us to stick to our agreed-upon budget for this project." Clarity around your limits creates safety and trust in the relationship.

Clarity isn't about being rigid—it's about being truthful and direct about what matters to you.

2. Compassion

Clarity is essential, but it must be paired with compassion. Compassion means bringing empathy and kindness to your interactions, recognizing that both you and your partner are human beings with vulnerabilities.

When communicating boundaries, compassion looks like:

- **Patience and grace**: Recognizing that changing habits takes time, and offering patience when missteps happen.

- **Acknowledging your partner's feelings**: Even if you disagree, acknowledge their perspective. "I see that you feel frustrated when I need alone time. I get that."

- **Openness to compromise**: Look for win-win solutions that honor both people's needs. "I know you want to go to that party. How about we go for an hour, and then spend some time alone together afterward?"

- **Repairing ruptures**: When communication breaks down, apologize and recommit to doing better. "I'm sorry for snapping earlier. I was feeling stressed, and it wasn't fair to take it out on you."

Compassion isn't about sacrificing your needs—it's about approaching difficult conversations with care for yourself and your partner.

3. Curiosity

The final key is curiosity. Curiosity means seeking to understand your partner's perspective with openness and a genuine desire to learn.

When approaching boundary conversations, curiosity might involve:

- **Asking questions**: Rather than assuming, ask questions to gain clarity. "Can you tell me more about what you were feeling when I said I needed space?"

- **Listening deeply**: Tune in fully to what your partner is saying without distractions or planning your response.

- **Being open to growth**: See conversations as opportunities to learn more about yourself, your partner, and your relationship.

- **Seeking to understand**: Shift your focus from being right to understanding where your partner is coming from. "Help me understand your point of view."

Curiosity helps break down defensiveness and opens space for collaborative problem-solving. It transforms boundary conversations into moments of connection and discovery rather than conflict.

· · · · **·** · **●** · **●** · · ·

Putting It All Together

The Three C's—**Clarity, Compassion, and Curiosity**—form the foundation of boundary-supporting communication. When you bring these qualities to your conversations, you create a space for deeper understanding and mutual respect. And while no communication will ever be perfect, practicing these skills over time will help you and your partner navigate challenges with grace.

The key is to keep showing up for these conversations with an open heart, even when it's difficult. Every time you choose to communicate with clarity, compassion, and curiosity, you strengthen the bond between you and your partner.

And remember, if you struggle with communication, it's okay to seek help. Couples therapy, workshops, and books on communication can all provide support. The goal is to keep learning and growing, trusting that loving, honest dialogue can transform your relationships.

So, take a deep breath, grab your partner's metaphorical hand, and step onto the dance floor of communication. You've got everything you need to move with clarity, compassion, and curiosity.

Workbook Exercise: Communication Check-In

Alright, time to put those communication skills to the test! In this exercise, you and your partner will have the opportunity to practice the Three C's of Boundary-Supporting Communication: Clarity, Compassion, and Curiosity. Think of it like a dance rehearsal—a chance to try out some new moves, find your rhythm, and maybe even have a few laughs along the way. And don't worry, no actual dancing required (unless you're feeling particularly inspired!).

Step 1: Set the Stage

First things first, create a safe and comfortable space for your communication practice. Find a time when you can talk without distractions or interruptions (yes, that means putting your phones on silent and telling the kids/roommates/pets that mommy and daddy are having "grown-up time").
You might even want to set the mood with some soft lighting, cozy pillows, or your favorite calming playlist. Think of it as creating your very own "communication love nest." Ooh la la!

Step 2: Choose Your Topic

Next, decide on a boundary-related topic you'd like to discuss. This could be something you've been struggling with in your relationship, or a hypothetical scenario you'd like to practice navigating.

Some ideas to get you started:

- Discussing expectations around alone time and togetherness

- Navigating differences in tidiness and household chores

- Setting limits around work hours and availability

- Expressing needs for physical affection and intimacy

- Managing family obligations and holiday plans

Feel free to get creative and choose a topic that feels relevant and meaningful to your relationship. And remember, the goal isn't to solve all your problems in one conversation—it's simply to practice communicating with clarity, compassion, and curiosity.

Step 3: Take Turns Sharing

Now it's time to put the Three C's into action! Take turns sharing your thoughts, feelings, and needs related to the chosen topic, using the following prompts as a guide:

Clarity:

- I feel... (name your emotion)

- I need... (state your boundary or request)

- I would like... (make a specific suggestion)

Compassion:

- I understand that you... (acknowledge your partner's perspective)

- I appreciate... (express gratitude or recognition)

- I'm sorry for... (take responsibility for your part)

Curiosity:

- Can you tell me more about... (ask an open-ended question)

- What do you need... (inquire about your partner's needs)

- How can we... (invite collaboration and problem-solving)

As you share, try to speak slowly and calmly, making eye contact and using "I" statements. And don't forget to breathe! If you start to feel triggered or defensive, take a moment to pause, reconnect with your intention to listen and understand.

Step 4: Practice Active Listening

While your partner is sharing, your job is to practice active listening. This means giving them your full attention and presence, without interrupting, judging, or planning your response.

Some active listening tips:

- Make eye contact and nod to show you're engaged

- Reflect back what you've heard to ensure understanding ("What I'm hearing is...")

- Ask clarifying questions to deepen your comprehension ("Can you say more about...?")

- Validate your partner's experience, even if you disagree ("I can see why you would feel that way.")

- Express empathy and care ("That sounds really challenging. I'm here for you.")

And if you find your mind wandering to your grocery list or that funny meme you saw earlier, gently redirect your attention back to your partner. Listening is a skill that takes practice, just like any other!

Step 5: Debrief and Celebrate

Once you've both had a chance to share and listen, take a moment to debrief and celebrate your communication efforts. You might ask each other:

- What went well in our conversation?

- What felt challenging or uncomfortable?

- What did we learn about ourselves or each other?

- How can we continue to practice and improve our communication skills?

And don't forget to acknowledge the courage and vulnerability it takes to show up for these conversations. You might even want to do a little victory dance or high-five to celebrate your progress (silly voices and gestures encouraged!).

Remember, the goal is not perfection, but practice. Every conversation is an opportunity to learn, grow, and deepen your connection.

So keep showing up, keep trying, and keep laughing along the way. With the Three C's as your guide, you've got everything you need to communicate your way to a love that lasts.

CHAPTER SIX

HANDLE THE PUSHBACK: HOW TO STAND STRONG WHEN BOUNDARIES ARE TESTED

So, you've done the hard work of getting clear on your boundaries. You've communicated them to your partner with clarity, compassion, and curiosity. You're feeling pretty good about this whole boundary-setting thing.

And then... it happens. Your partner pushes back. They question your needs, argue with your limits, or flat-out ignore your requests. Suddenly, all that boundary clarity starts to feel a little murky.

Maybe your partner says something like:

- "Do you really need that much alone time? I thought you enjoyed spending time with me."

- "I don't see why I should have to text you every time I'm running late. You're being controlling."

- "You're too sensitive. I was just joking when I made that comment about your weight."

Ouch. Pushback can sting. It leaves you feeling confused, defensive, maybe even questioning whether your boundaries are too much. Are you being unreasonable? Too demanding? Too sensitive?

But here's the thing: Pushback is a normal part of the boundary-setting process. It doesn't mean you're doing something wrong—in fact, it usually means you're doing something right!

Think about it. If you've been accommodating and self-sacrificing in your relationship for a while, your partner may be used to that dynamic. So when you start setting clearer limits and advocating for your needs, it's natural for them to feel a little unsettled.

Of course, that doesn't make pushback easy to handle. It can be tempting to cave in, to revert back to your old people-pleasing ways just to keep the peace. But learning to stand firm in your boundaries—even when your partner resists—is crucial for creating healthy, balanced relationships.

In this chapter, we'll explore how to navigate pushback with strength and compassion. You'll learn strategies for staying grounded in your truth, even when your partner challenges you. And you'll discover how these moments of friction can lead to deeper understanding and growth in your relationship.

So take a deep breath, summon your inner boundary warrior, and let's dive in.

. . . ● . ● . ● . . .

Why Pushback Happens (And What It Really Means)

Before we jump into specific strategies, let's take a moment to understand why pushback happens in the first place. What's going on when your partner resists or challenges your boundaries?

While every situation is unique, pushback often stems from one or more of the following:

- **Fear of change:** If your relationship has operated a certain way for a long time, any disruption can feel scary. Your partner may fear losing the comfort of the old dynamic, even if it wasn't healthy.

- **Unmet needs:** Pushback can sometimes be a sign that your partner feels their needs aren't being met. If they're feeling neglected or disconnected, they might resist your boundary in an attempt to get closer.

- **Differing expectations:** Your partner may have different ideas about what's "normal" in relationships, shaped by their upbringing, culture, or past experiences.

- **Ego and entitlement:** If your partner is used to getting their way, they might see your boundaries as a threat to their control or sense of entitlement.

- **Genuine confusion or concern:** Sometimes, pushback comes from a place of misunderstanding. Your partner may not fully grasp why your boundary is important to you and may need more clarity.

Understanding the root of pushback helps you approach it with more insight. Instead of getting caught up in the surface resistance, you can tune in to what's really going on beneath it. This doesn't mean you need to accommodate their pushback, but it does help you respond with empathy while standing firm in your truth.

Some Useful Reframes for Pushback

- **Pushback is not a sign that your boundaries are wrong.** It's a sign that you're inviting a new, healthier dynamic into your relationship.

- **Pushback is not a personal attack,** even if it feels like one. Often, it's a reflection of your partner's fears or unmet needs.

- **Pushback is not the end of the conversation.** It's an opportunity for deeper dialogue and understanding between you and your partner.

With these reframes in mind, let's look at some common pushback scenarios and strategies for responding with both strength and compassion.

• • • **•** • **•** • • •

Pushback Scenarios and Responses

Scenario 1: Questioning Your Needs

Your boundary: "I need some alone time to recharge after work. Please don't take it personally if I need to retreat to my room for a bit."

Pushback: "Why do you need so much alone time? I thought we were supposed to enjoy spending time together."

Response:

- "I hear that you're feeling a little hurt by my need for alone time. I want to reassure you that it has nothing to do with how much I care about you. Taking some solo time to recharge actually helps me show up as a better, more present partner for you. Can we brainstorm some ways to make sure we're both getting our needs met?"

- "I understand this is a shift from how we used to do things. It might take some getting used to, but I believe it will be so good for our relationship in the long run. I'm not rejecting you, I'm investing in my own well-being so that I can be the best version of myself for us."

Scenario 2: Accusing You of Being Controlling

Your boundary: "If you're going to be more than 15 minutes late, please let me know. I worry when I don't hear from you."

Pushback: "Why do I have to check in with you every time I'm running late? You're being controlling."

Response:

- "I can see how my request might have come across as controlling, but that's not my intention at all. I'm not trying to track your every move, I just feel anxious when I'm left wondering what happened to you. Is there a way we could compromise on this that would help us both feel respected and cared for?"

- "You're right, I'm not your parent and I don't want to control you. But as your partner, your wellbeing matters to me. When you're running late, a quick heads up helps me not worry and frees me up to focus on my own stuff. It's about consideration, not control. How can we find a middle ground here?"

Scenario 3: Invalidating Your Feelings

Your boundary: "Some of your jokes about my body make me feel uncomfortable. I need you to stop commenting on my weight."

Pushback: "Come on, I'm just joking. You're too sensitive."

Response:

- "I know you don't intend to hurt me with your jokes. But the reality is, they do impact my self-esteem, regardless of your intent. I'm not asking you to walk on eggshells, I'm asking you to be mindful of a sensitive topic for me. Can we find a way to joke around that doesn't make either of us feel bad about ourselves?"

- "I hear that you feel like you can't say anything right. That must be really frustrating. And I imagine it's equally frustrating for you when I get upset by something you see as harmless. I don't think either of us wants to hurt or silence the other. How can we learn to communicate in a way that helps us both feel heard and respected?"

• • • • • • • • • •

When Pushback Crosses the Line

Sometimes pushback goes beyond resistance and crosses into unhealthy territory, such as:

- **Emotional manipulation**: Your partner uses guilt, shame, or withdrawal of affection to pressure you into abandoning your boundaries. They may say things like "If you really loved me, you would..." or give you the silent treatment when you assert a limit.

- **Gaslighting**: Your partner denies your reality or makes you question your own perceptions and instincts. They may tell you that you're overreacting, being irrational, or imagining things when you try to assert a boundary.

- **Boundary steamrolling**: Your partner consistently ignores or overrides your clearly stated boundaries. They may apologize and promise to do better, but their actions don't match their words.

- **Verbal or physical intimidation**: Your partner uses aggressive language, tone, or body language to make you feel unsafe or afraid to assert your boundaries. They may yell, threaten, or get in your physical space when you try to set a limit.

If your partner's pushback involves any of these behaviors, it may be a sign that the relationship needs to be re-evaluated. You deserve to have your boundaries respected, and no relationship is worth compromising your well-being.

· · · ● · ● · ● · ● · ·

Boundaries as Opportunities for Growth

While pushback can be challenging, it's also an opportunity for growth—both for you and your relationship. Every time you stand firm in your boundaries, you're reinforcing your self-worth and strengthening your relationship with yourself. And each time you and your partner work through boundary friction with honesty and care, you're building a stronger foundation for your relationship.

So when pushback happens, remind yourself: this is important work. You're not just setting boundaries—you're creating a relationship where both of you can thrive.

Workbook Exercise: Boundary Defender Roleplay

Alright, boundary warriors! It's time to put your pushback-handling skills to the test. In this exercise, you'll have the chance to roleplay some common boundary pushback scenarios and practice responding with both strength and compassion. Think of it like a training montage in a superhero movie—you're gearing up to face the villains of boundary violations, and this is your chance to hone your superpowers of clear communication and unshakable self-worth. Cue the epic music!

Step 1: Choose Your Scenarios

First, choose 3-5 boundary pushback scenarios that feel relevant to your life and relationships. You can use the examples from the chapter, or come up with your own based on your experiences.

Some ideas to get you started:

1. Your partner complains that your need for alone time is a sign that you don't care about the relationship.

2. Your friend gets defensive when you ask them to stop making jokes at your expense.

3. Your family member guilt-trips you for setting a limit around how often you can babysit their kids.

4. Your coworker accuses you of being selfish for not taking on extra projects outside your job description.

5. Your partner gives you the silent treatment after you say no to a request that makes you uncomfortable.

Feel free to get creative and choose scenarios that reflect the unique challenges and dynamics of your own life. The more specific and realistic, the better!

Step 2: Craft Your Responses

For each scenario you've chosen, take some time to craft a response that feels authentic and aligned for you. Remember the key principles from the chapter:

- Stay grounded in your truth and the validity of your needs

- Speak from a place of "I" statements and personal ownership

- Make space to understand your partner's perspective and feelings

- Balance firmness and compassion, assertiveness and empathy

Here's a quick template you can use to structure your responses:

1. Acknowledge your partner's feelings or perspective: "I hear that you feel [emotion] when I [set boundary]. That must be [validating statement]."

2. Reaffirm your boundary and its importance to you: "At the same time, [boundary] is really important to me because [reason]. It's not about [misinterpretation], it's about [real intention]."

3. Invite a collaborative conversation: "I care about your needs too, and I want to find a way to honor both of our needs. Can we [specific request for collaboration or compromise]?"

For example, let's say your scenario is: Your partner complains that your need for alone time is a sign that you don't care about the relationship.

Your response might sound something like:

"I hear that you feel hurt and worried when I take alone time. That must be a scary feeling, to wonder if I'm pulling away. At the same time, taking solo time to recharge is really important to me because it helps me show up as a better, more present partner. It's not about me not caring, it's about me taking care of myself so I can be my best self for us. I care about your needs for connection too, and I want to find a way to honor both of our needs. Can we look at our schedules together and carve out some dedicated quality time, so we both feel nourished?"

Take your time crafting responses that feel true and resonant for you. And remember, there's no one "perfect" thing to say—the goal is simply to practice showing up for yourself with clarity and compassion.

Step 3: Rehearse and Refine

Now it's time to take your responses from the page to the stage! Find a quiet, private space where you can rehearse your boundary comebacks out loud.

You might enlist a friend to play the role of your boundary-pushing partner, or you can simply imagine the scenario in your mind's eye. The important thing is to get comfortable expressing your truth out loud, even if it feels a bit awkward at first.

As you rehearse, pay attention to your body language and tone of voice. Notice if you're shrinking or apologizing, and see if you can stand a little taller, speak a little more firmly. Embody the energy of a powerful, compassionate boundary-setter.

Feel free to tweak and refine your responses as you go. If something doesn't quite land right, play around with different words or phrasings until you find what feels authentic for you.

And don't be afraid to infuse a little playfulness into your practice! You might give your boundary superhero self a cheeky name (Captain Compassionate Limit-Setter, perhaps?), or do a celebratory dance after each successful comeback. The more fun and lightness you can bring to this practice, the easier it will be to implement in real life.

Step 4: Take It to the Real World

You've done the inner work, you've rehearsed your heart out—now it's time to take your boundary badassery out into the wild!

The next time you encounter a real-life boundary pushback scenario, take a deep breath, channel your inner superhero, and speak your truth with clarity and care. Remember, you've got this. You've been training for this moment.

And if it doesn't go perfectly, that's okay! Boundary-setting is a lifelong practice, not a one-time performance. Every conversation is an opportunity to learn, grow, and refine your approach.

So keep showing up, keep speaking up, and keep shining bright. The world needs your unique brand of boundary brilliance.

Reflection Prompts

After practicing your boundary defenders, take a moment to reflect on the experience. Jot down your responses to these prompts in your trusty boundary journal:

1. What felt empowering or natural about standing up for my boundaries? What felt challenging or uncomfortable?

2. What old stories or beliefs about my worth and my right to have needs came up as I was practicing? How can I rewrite those stories into ones of empowerment and self-love?

3. What do I want to remember the next time I face boundary pushback in real life? What inner resources can I draw upon to support me in those moments?

4. How might my relationships transform if I consistently show up for my boundaries with clarity and compassion? What would it feel like to be that grounded and self-honoring?

Remember, every reflection, every rehearsal, every real-life boundary stand is a revolutionary act. You're not just standing up for yourself—you're part of a larger movement to create a world where everyone's needs and limits are honored.

PART IV: ALL ABOUT INTIMACY: BOUNDARIES IN THE BEDROOM AND BEYOND

CHAPTER SEVEN

BEDROOM BOUNDARIES: KEEP IT SPICY WITHOUT GETTING STEAMY OVER FIGHTS

The bedroom... The boudoir... The love nest... The place where magic happens... and sometimes, where boundaries get blurred.

Navigating boundaries in the context of physical intimacy can be particularly challenging. Sex and touch are vulnerable, emotionally charged territories, so it's no wonder that misunderstandings and mixed signals happen often.

Maybe you've experienced some of these boundary bumps in your own bedroom:

- You're not in the mood for sex but feel guilty saying no to your partner.

- Your partner introduces a new sexual desire that makes you uncomfortable.

- You feel pressure to have sex more (or less) often than you'd like.

- Your partner touches you in a way that turns you off, but you don't know how to speak up.

Sound familiar? If so, you're not alone. Many couples struggle with how to communicate their sexual needs, wants, and limits clearly and confidently.

But here's the good news: setting boundaries in the bedroom doesn't have to kill the vibe. In fact, it can make your sex life even more satisfying for both you and your partner.

When you're able to express your authentic desires and feel safe saying no to what doesn't feel right, you create the conditions for real intimacy and deeper sexual connection. You can relax, let go, and fully enjoy the experience, knowing your boundaries will be respected.

In this chapter, we'll explore how to set and maintain boundaries around sex and physical touch in ways that deepen desire and strengthen your romantic bond. You'll learn how to get clear on your sexual needs and limits, communicate them with confidence, and navigate common challenges that arise in the bedroom.

· · · · ● · ● · ● · ● · ● · ·

Why Bedroom Boundaries Matter

Sexual boundaries are fundamentally about consent and safety. They affirm that each person has full authority over their own body and sexual experience. By setting clear boundaries, you and your partner create an environment where enthusiastic consent is the foundation of your intimate life.

Boundaries aren't just about preventing harm, though—they also pave the way for deeper pleasure and connection. When you feel safe and respected, you're able to fully engage in the moment, rather than worrying about having your boundaries crossed.

Imagine trying to enjoy a sexual encounter while feeling tense or uncomfortable. It's impossible to relax and savor the experience when you're mentally managing your discomfort.

On the other hand, when you trust that your boundaries will be honored, you're free to get creative with your sexual expression. You can communicate your desires openly, explore new experiences, and immerse yourself in the joy of giving and receiving pleasure.

In this way, boundaries actually create more space for sexual freedom and exploration. They give you and your partner the safety net you need to let your guard down and be fully present in the moment.

· · · ● · ● · ● · ● · ·

Getting Clear on Your Sexual Boundaries

Before you can communicate your boundaries with a partner, it's important to get clear on what they actually are. Many people haven't taken the time to reflect on their sexual needs, wants, and limits.

Self-reflection is a key part of boundary-setting. By tuning into your own desires and discomforts, you can better understand your unique sexual truth.

Here are some prompts to help you explore your sexual boundaries:

1. What kind of touch feels good to me? What kind of touch makes me uncomfortable?

2. What sexual activities do I enjoy? Which ones am I indifferent to or dislike?

3. How often do I want to have sex, and what factors influence my desire?

4. What helps me feel safe and respected during sexual interactions? What makes me feel disrespected?

5. Are there any sexual acts that are completely off-limits for me?

6. What are my secret sexual desires? What do I wish to experience more of?

You might find it helpful to journal your thoughts or revisit these questions periodically. Sexual boundaries can shift over time, so it's important to stay attuned to what feels right for you.

Remember, your sexual needs and boundaries are valid—period. There's no need to justify or apologize for them.

• • • ● • ● • ● • • •

Communicating Your Boundaries With a Partner

Once you've clarified your sexual boundaries, the next step is communicating them to your partner. This can feel vulnerable, but it's an essential part of building trust and intimacy.

Here are some tips for boundary conversations around sex:

- **Choose the right time and place.** Have the conversation when you're both calm and relaxed, ideally outside of a sexual encounter.

- Choose the right time and place. Have the conversation when you're both calm, well-rested, and not under the influence of substances. Try to pick a neutral location where you can talk without distractions or interruptions.

- Use "I" statements to express your needs and limits. For example, "I feel most comfortable with monogamy" instead of "You better not cheat on me." This helps your partner understand your perspective without feeling attacked.

- Be specific and direct. Avoid vague statements like "I don't know..." or "Maybe we could try..." Instead, state your boundaries clearly and confidently: "I'm not interested in anal sex" or "I need you to ask before initiating touch."

- Express your desires, not just your limits. Share what kind of touch and sexual activities you do enjoy, so your partner has a clear sense of how to please you. For example, "I really love it when you kiss my neck softly."

- Listen to your partner's needs and boundaries with curiosity and compassion. Make space for them to share their desires and limits too, without judgment or defensiveness.

- Be willing to negotiate and find creative solutions. Not all boundaries are hard lines in the sand. There may be room for compromise and experimentation. For example, "I'm not comfortable with penetration right now, but I would love to explore oral sex."

- Revisit the conversation regularly. Sexual needs and boundaries can shift over time, so it's important to keep communicating about them. Make boundary check-ins a regular part of your relationship maintenance.

By discussing boundaries openly, you and your partner can co-create a sexual relationship that feels good for both of you.

$$\cdots\bullet\cdot\bullet\cdot\bullet\cdot\bullet\cdots$$

Handling Boundary Bumps and Violations

Even with clear communication, boundary bumps and misunderstandings happen. Maybe your partner unintentionally crosses a line in the heat of the moment, or maybe you realize mid-encounter that something isn't feeling right.

Here's how to handle those moments:

- Speak up as soon as you feel uncomfortable. Don't wait until the end of the sexual encounter to voice your boundary. A simple "stop," "pause," or "not there" can communicate that something isn't okay.

- Take a deep breath and check in with your body. Notice what sensations and emotions are coming up for you. Are you feeling tense, anxious, or disconnected? Or relaxed, safe, and present?

- Express your needs and limits clearly and calmly. For example, "I'm not comfortable with that position. Can we try something else?" or "I need a moment to slow down and reconnect with my body."

- If your partner respects your boundary and adjusts their behavior, acknowledge and appreciate their effort. For example, "Thank you for listening and changing course. I feel much safer now."

- If your partner ignores or dismisses your boundary, it's okay to end the sexual encounter. You might say something like, "I don't feel safe continuing right now. I need to stop and talk about what just happened."

- In the aftermath of a boundary violation, take time to process your feelings. You might journal, talk to a trusted friend, or seek support from a therapist. Remember, your feelings are valid and it's okay to take space to care for yourself.

- When you're ready, have a follow-up conversation with your partner about what happened. Use "I" statements to express how the boundary violation impacted you, and brainstorm together how to prevent similar situations in the future.

Boundary violations are often unintentional, but addressing them in the moment helps prevent misunderstandings from escalating.

· · ● · ● · ● · · ·

Cultivating a Culture of Consent

Setting and honoring boundaries in the bedroom is about more than just individual interactions—it's about creating a culture of consent and respect in your relationship.

Here are a few ways to cultivate consent beyond the bedroom:

- **Make boundary check-ins a regular part of your relationship.** Ask each other about needs and limits regularly, not just during sex.

- **Support each other in saying no.** Create an atmosphere where both partners feel empowered to decline without guilt or pressure.

- **Model consent in everyday interactions.** Whether it's asking before hugging or offering space when needed, practicing consent creates a foundation of mutual respect.

By fostering a culture of consent, you're building a relationship where both partners feel respected, heard, and valued.

Workbook Exercise: Intimacy Map

Alright, intrepid explorers of intimacy! It's time to dive deep into the lush landscape of your erotic desires and boundaries. In this exercise, you'll create a detailed "map" of your sexual needs, wants, and limits, and practice communicating them with a partner.

Think of it like a treasure hunt for your authentic sexual truth. You'll be unearthing the gems of your yeses, the pearls of your maybes, and the precious artifacts of your no's. And along the way, you'll be building the skills to share your discoveries with a trusted co-adventurer.

So grab your imaginary fedora and bullwhip (or whatever sexy archeologist gear gets you in the mood), and let's get mapping!

Part 1: Solo Exploration

First, set aside some solo time to get curious about your sexual inner world. Find a comfortable, private space where you can reflect without distractions. You might light some candles, put on some sensual music, or do whatever helps you feel relaxed and open.

Then, grab a journal or some paper and start free-writing your responses to the following prompts:

1. What kind of touch feels most delicious and arousing to me? Where do I like to be touched, and with what kind of pressure or sensation?

2. What sexual activities light me up and leave me hungry for more? Which ones feel "meh" or actively turn me off?

3. What helps me feel safe and respected during sexual encounters? What makes me feel unsafe or disrespected?

4. How often do I like to have sex or engage in intimate touch? What factors impact my desire and availability?

5. What are my hard "no"s when it comes to sex—the activities or dynamics that are completely off-limits for me?

6. What are my secret sexual fantasies and desires? What do I long to experience in my erotic life, even if it feels edgy or vulnerable to admit?

As you write, try to stay curious and non-judgmental. There's no right or wrong here—the goal is simply to get to know your erotic self more intimately. If certain prompts bring up discomfort or resistance, be extra gentle with yourself. Honor whatever arises, and know that you're doing brave work by showing up for this self-exploration.

Once you've finished free-writing, take a look at what you've uncovered. What patterns or themes do you notice? What feels most important or salient to you? What surprised you?

Take a few moments to distill your discoveries into a "legend" for your intimacy map. You might create categories like:

- Green light (Full yes! Activities that I love and crave)

- Yellow light (Maybe/depends. Activities that I might enjoy under certain circumstances)

- Red light (Hard no. Activities that are completely off-limits)

You could also include categories for things like:

- Ideal frequency of sex/intimacy

- Specific boundaries around certain body parts or types of touch

- Conditions that help you feel safe and relaxed (e.g. lights on or off, music, certain positions)

- Sexual fantasies you'd like to explore more

Get creative and make your legend as detailed and specific as feels helpful for you. And remember, this is a living document. Your sexual boundaries and desires may shift and evolve over time, so plan to revisit your intimacy map regularly and make updates as needed.

Part 2: Courageous Communication

Now that you've got a clearer sense of your own erotic landscape, it's time to practice sharing your map with a partner. This might feel vulnerable or awkward at first, but remember—your boundaries are a beautiful part of your sexual truth. By communicating them clearly and confidently, you're inviting deeper intimacy and connection.

Here are some tips for sharing your intimacy map:

1. Choose a time and place where you both feel comfortable and relaxed. This probably isn't a conversation to have in the heat of the moment, but rather during a quieter, more clothed moment.

2. Let your partner know that you've been doing some reflection on your sexual needs and boundaries, and that you'd like to share what you've discovered. Invite them to listen with curiosity and openness.

3. Using your intimacy map as a guide, share your green, yellow, and red light zones. Be specific and direct, using "I" statements to express your desires and limits. For example: "I really love it when you kiss my neck and ears. That's a total green light for me." "I'm open to trying anal play, but I need to take it really slow and use a lot of lube. That's more of a yellow light activity." "I'm not comfortable with any kind of breath play or choking. That's a hard red light for me."

4. If you feel comfortable, share some of your sexual fantasies or desires. Let your partner know what turns you on and what you'd like to explore together.

5. Invite your partner to share their own intimacy map, if they feel comfortable. Listen with the same curiosity and openness that you've asked for.

6. Together, look for areas of overlap and mutual interest. Where do your green lights align? What yellow light activities might you explore together, with clear communication and consent? Celebrate the points of connection and get excited about the adventures ahead!

7. Also look for areas of difference or potential conflict. Where do your boundaries or desires diverge? How can you navigate these differences with care and creativity? For example, if you have different ideal frequencies for sex, you might brainstorm ways to stay intimately connected even when you're not having intercourse (sensual massage, making out, cuddle time). Or if you have different comfort levels with a certain activity, you might discuss ways to build trust and safety, or find alternative activities that feel good for both of you.

Remember, the goal here isn't to have perfectly aligned intimacy maps, but rather to understand and honor each other's unique erotic truths. By approaching your differences with curiosity and compassion, you can find creative ways to expand your shared comfort zone and keep your sexual connection thriving.

Part 3: Intimacy In Action

With your intimacy maps as a guide, you can now bring more conscious communication and boundary-setting to your sexual play. Here are some ways to keep your maps alive in the bedroom (and beyond!):

1. Before getting frisky, do a quick check-in about your green, yellow, and red lights for that encounter. Share any relevant factors (like tiredness or stress levels) that might be impacting your desires or limits.

2. As things heat up, keep communicating! Let your partner know what feels good ("Ooh, yes, keep doing that!") and what doesn't ("Actually, can we switch positions? This one isn't working for me."). Remember, feedback is a gift that helps your partner love you better.

3. If you're exploring something new or edgy, take it slow and check in frequently. Use a simple scale (like 1-5) to share your comfort and arousal levels, and make sure you have a safe word in case you need to stop.

4. When you're finished, take a few minutes to debrief and share appreciations. What felt especially good? What do you want to try again next time? Celebrating your successes (and learning from your "oops" moments) helps keep your intimacy muscles strong and flexible.

Above all, remember that boundary-setting is a life-long practice, not a one-time deal. Keep revisiting your intimacy map, keep talking to your partner, and keep honoring your authentic sexual self.

With every courageous conversation and every consensual cuddle, you're helping to create a world where every body and every desire is treated with care.

CHAPTER EIGHT

EMOTIONAL BOUNDARIES: LET'S GET CLOSER BY DRAWING THE RIGHT LINES

Emotions—those wild, unpredictable forces of human nature—are what make relationships rich, meaningful, and sometimes, downright challenging. At their best, emotions can bring us closer together, deepen our understanding, and enhance our connection. But when left unchecked or poorly managed, they can turn relationships into emotional rollercoasters, creating confusion, resentment, and distance.

Navigating the emotional landscape of a relationship can sometimes feel like walking through a field of landmines. You're not sure what might set off a chain reaction of hurt feelings, defensiveness, or emotional shutdowns. It can be exhausting and, quite frankly, terrifying. But what if I told you there's a way to defuse those landmines before they explode? A way to nurture deep intimacy and trust, while still protecting your own emotional well-being?

That's where emotional boundaries come in.

Emotional boundaries are the invisible lines we draw between our emotional world and the emotional world of others. They help define where we end and our partner begins, allowing us to protect our feelings, honor our needs, and take responsibility for our own emotional state without taking on the emotional baggage of others.

When we have healthy emotional boundaries, we can:

- Feel our feelings fully without being overwhelmed by them.

- Communicate our needs and desires clearly and directly, without expecting our partner to read our mind.

- Take responsibility for our own emotional well-being rather than relying on others to "fix" us or make us happy.

- Allow our partner the space to have their own emotions and experiences without feeling the need to control or fix them.

- Navigate conflicts with greater grace and resilience, staying anchored to our core selves instead of getting swept up in emotional drama.

In short, emotional boundaries are the secret sauce to maintaining a healthy sense of self within relationships. They allow us to love fully without losing ourselves, to care deeply without being consumed.

But here's the thing: setting emotional boundaries doesn't come naturally for most of us. Many of us grew up in families where emotional boundaries were unclear, blurry, or non-existent. We were taught, directly or indirectly, that our worth depended on pleasing others, caretaking, or sacrificing our own needs for the sake of harmony.

So, if you struggle with emotional boundaries, you're not alone. The good news is that you can learn to set and maintain them, no matter how messy your emotional history may be.

Common Emotional Boundary Challenges

Emotional boundary struggles can show up in several different forms, but here are some of the most common:

1. Enmeshment: This happens when you become so wrapped up in your partner's emotions that you lose touch with your own. Their moods, feelings, and problems take over your emotional world, and you may find yourself walking on eggshells or constantly trying to manage their feelings.

2. Codependency: This is when your sense of self-worth becomes intertwined with your partner's approval. You rely on them to make you feel okay, and you may feel anxious, empty, or lost when you're not receiving validation from them.

3. Emotional Reactivity: Without clear boundaries, your partner's emotions can trigger intense reactions in you, leading to fights, withdrawal, or feelings of being overwhelmed. You may take everything personally or find yourself constantly on edge.

4. Lack of Differentiation: Differentiation is the ability to remain emotionally connected to your partner while still maintaining your individuality. When boundaries are lacking, you may feel like you're losing your identity within the relationship.

Why Emotional Boundaries Matter

Emotional boundaries aren't about building walls between you and your partner. They're about creating a sense of emotional sovereignty—being able to hold space for your own feelings while still being empathetic and supportive of your partner's. Healthy emotional boundaries allow you to be in a relationship without feeling responsible for your partner's emotions or allowing their emotional state to overwhelm yours.

Boundaries are an essential part of self-care, and they are vital to creating a relationship that is both deeply intimate and mutually respectful. They give you the emotional space you need to take care of yourself, which, in turn, makes you a better partner. Think of boundaries as a way to create emotional breathing room. They're what allow you to stay connected without getting emotionally suffocated.

• • • • ● • ● • • •

Busting the Myths About Emotional Boundaries

Let's clear up a few common misconceptions that can keep us from setting emotional boundaries:

Myth #1: Boundaries are selfish.

Truth: Boundaries are a way of respecting yourself. By taking care of your emotional needs, you're actually better able to show up for others in a healthy, sustainable way.

Myth #2: Boundaries are rigid and controlling.

Truth: Boundaries are flexible and adaptable. They're not about control; they're about protecting your emotional well-being. You can set boundaries while still being open to compromise and collaboration.

Myth #3: Boundaries are only necessary when there's conflict.

Truth: Boundaries are important all the time. They're not just for crisis management; they help create healthy emotional dynamics in everyday life.

Myth #4: If I set boundaries, my partner will feel rejected.

Truth: Healthy boundaries actually make relationships stronger. When both partners feel emotionally safe and respected, they're able to connect more deeply.

Myth #5: Once boundaries are set, they don't need to be revisited.

Truth: Boundaries evolve. As you grow and your relationship changes, you'll need to regularly check in with your boundaries to ensure they're still serving you.

How to Set Emotional Boundaries

Setting emotional boundaries isn't a one-time conversation. It's a process that involves self-awareness, communication, and practice. Here are some practical steps to help you set and maintain healthy emotional boundaries in your relationships:

1. Get Clear on Your Own Emotional Needs

Before you can set boundaries, you need to know what you're protecting. Spend some time reflecting on your emotional needs. What makes you feel safe and supported in your relationship? What triggers emotional overwhelm or discomfort? Understanding your own emotional landscape is the first step in setting boundaries that honor your needs.

2. Communicate with Clarity and Compassion

Once you've identified your needs, the next step is to communicate them to your partner. Use "I" statements to express how you feel and what you need, without blaming or accusing your partner. For example, instead of saying, "You're always dumping your problems on me," you could say, "I've been feeling overwhelmed lately, and I need some space to process my own emotions before I can be fully present for you."

3. Stay Grounded in Your Boundaries

Emotional boundaries are only effective if you enforce them consistently. This means standing firm in your boundaries, even when it feels uncomfortable. It's natural for people to push back when boundaries are set, especially if they're used to you absorbing their emotions or taking responsibility for their feelings. It's important to stay grounded and remind yourself that your emotional well-being is a priority.

4. Practice Emotional Regulation

Setting boundaries doesn't mean you won't feel triggered or upset by your partner's emotions. The key is learning how to regulate your own emotions so you don't react impulsively or emotionally shut down. Practices like deep breathing, mindfulness, and journaling can help you stay centered when emotions are running high.

5. Revisit and Adjust Your Boundaries as Needed

Relationships are dynamic, and so are emotional boundaries. As your relationship evolves, your boundaries may need to shift. Make it a habit to check in with yourself and your partner regularly to ensure your boundaries are still serving both of you. Open, ongoing communication is key to keeping your emotional boundaries healthy and effective.

• • • ● • ● • ● • • •

Examples of Healthy Emotional Boundaries in Action

Let's look at a few real-life scenarios to see how emotional boundaries can play out in practice:

Scenario 1: The Emotional Dump

Context: Your partner comes home from work in a terrible mood. They immediately start venting about their stressful day, unloading all their frustrations on you. You want to be supportive, but you're also feeling drained from your own day.

Unhealthy Response: You absorb your partner's emotions and start feeling just as stressed as they are. You take on their problems as your own, feeling responsible for making them feel better.

Healthy Boundary Response: You listen to your partner for a few minutes, then gently set a boundary: "I hear that you've had a tough day, and I want to be there for you, but I'm feeling a bit overwhelmed myself. Can we take a break and talk about this later, once we've both had some time to unwind?"

Scenario 2: The Silent Treatment

Context: You and your partner have a disagreement, and instead of addressing the issue, your partner shuts down and gives you the silent treatment. This leaves you feeling anxious and emotionally disconnected.

Unhealthy Response: You try to break the silence by apologizing, even if you don't think you did anything wrong, just to restore peace. You feel responsible for ending the conflict.

Healthy Boundary Response: You give your partner space to process their feelings while maintaining your emotional boundaries. "I understand that you need some time to cool off, and I respect that. I'm here when you're ready to talk, but I don't feel comfortable being shut out. Let's agree to come back to this when we're both ready."

Workbook Exercise: Emotional Check-In Chart

Alright, it's time to get up close and personal with your emotional boundaries! In this exercise, you'll create a personalized "Emotional Check-In Chart"—a tool for tracking your feelings, needs, and boundaries on a regular basis.

Think of it like a fitness tracker for your emotional well-being. Just like you might log your daily steps or water intake, this chart will help you stay attuned to your inner world and communicate your needs to your partner.

But don't worry, this isn't about perfection or rigidity. Your emotional boundaries are allowed to be messy, complex, and ever-evolving. This chart is simply a compassionate space to get curious about your own experience and practice expressing it with love.

So grab your favorite pen, put on some mood-setting music, and let's get emotionally charting!

Part 1: Identifying Your Emotional Needs and Triggers

Before you can communicate your emotional boundaries to your partner, you need to get clear on what they are for yourself. This first part of the exercise will help you tune into your own feelings, needs, and sensitivities.

Find a quiet, comfortable space where you can reflect without interruption. Take a few deep breaths and allow yourself to settle into the present moment. Then, consider the following prompts:

1. What emotions do I feel most often in my relationship? What triggers or situations tend to bring up these feelings?

2. What do I need to feel emotionally safe and secure in my relationship? What helps me feel seen, heard, and respected by my partner?

3. What emotional states or experiences do I find challenging or overwhelming? What pushes me outside my window of tolerance?

4. How do I typically cope with difficult emotions in my relationship? Do I tend to shut down, lash out, or seek reassurance from my partner?

5. What unmet needs or unhealed wounds might be influencing my emotional reactions and boundaries? What past experiences might be shaping my current triggers?

As you reflect on these questions, jot down any insights or patterns that emerge. Don't worry about having perfect answers—the goal is simply to deepen your self-awareness and compassion.

If certain prompts bring up difficult emotions or memories, be extra gentle with yourself. Consider reaching out to a trusted friend, therapist, or support group for additional processing and care.

Part 2: Creating Your Emotional Check-In Chart

Now that you have a clearer sense of your emotional landscape, it's time to create a tool for tracking and communicating your boundaries on a regular basis.

Grab a sheet of paper or open a new document on your computer. Create a chart with the following columns:

- Date/Time

- Emotion(s)

- Need(s)

- Boundary/Request

- Partner Response

- Self-Care Practice

Your chart will be unique to your own emotional needs and experiences. The key is to get in the habit of regularly checking in with yourself and communicating your boundaries to your partner in a clear, direct way.

Some tips for using your Emotional Check-In Chart:

- Try to fill it out at least once a day, or whenever you notice a strong emotion or boundary issue arising.

- Be as specific as possible when naming your emotions and needs. Instead of just writing "upset," try to pinpoint whether you're feeling "angry," "hurt," "scared," etc.

- Frame your boundary statements as clear, actionable requests, rather than criticisms or demands. Use "I" statements to own your experience.

- Notice how your partner responds to your boundary communication. Do they listen with empathy and respect? Do they get defensive or dismissive? This information can help you identify patterns and areas for growth in your relationship.

- Make sure to include a self-care practice for each check-in. This could be something small, like taking a few deep breaths, or something more involved, like going for a run or calling a supportive friend. The goal is to remind yourself that you have the tools to regulate your own emotions, independent of your partner.

Remember, your Emotional Check-In Chart is not a scorecard or a weapon. It's a compassionate tool for deepening your self-awareness, communicating your truth, and taking responsibility for your own well-being.

So use it with love, both for yourself and your partner. And trust that every check-in, every vulnerable share, every act of self-care, is strengthening your emotional boundary muscles.

Part 3: Reflecting and Integrating

After using your Emotional Check-In Chart for a week or two, take some time to reflect on your experience. Consider journaling about the following prompts:

1. What patterns or themes do I notice in my emotions and needs? Are there any triggers or situations that come up repeatedly?

2. How has communicating my boundaries directly impacted my relationship? Have I noticed any shifts in my partner's responsiveness or my own sense of emotional safety?

3. What has been challenging about this practice? What resistance or fears have come up for me around asserting my boundaries?

4. What has been rewarding or empowering about this practice? How has it enhanced my self-awareness, self-compassion, and relational intimacy?

5. What support or resources do I need to continue strengthening my emotional boundary skills? How can I prioritize my own emotional well-being moving forward?

As you reflect, celebrate every moment of growth and learning—even the messy, imperfect ones. Remember, boundary-setting is a lifelong practice, not a one-time achievement.

So keep showing up for yourself, one check-in at a time. Keep honoring your emotions, communicating your needs, and practicing radical self-care. Keep being the boundaried badass you were born to be.

And know that with every boundary you set, you're not only healing your own heart—you're helping to create a world where all emotions are valid, all needs are worthy, and all relationships are rooted in mutual care and respect.

Part V: Fighting Fair: Boundaries During Conflict

CHAPTER NINE

FIGHTING SMART: BOUNDARIES IN THE HEAT OF AN ARGUMENT

Conflict. Disagreements. Arguments. These are the inevitable moments when you and your partner find yourselves on opposite sides of an issue, with tempers flaring and emotions running high.

Let's be honest: it's not a matter of *if* conflicts will happen, but *when*. Even the healthiest, most loving relationships will encounter disagreements and differences from time to time. After all, you're two unique individuals trying to create a shared life. It's bound to get messy at some point.

But here's the thing: how you handle conflict can make or break your relationship in the long run. Do you approach disagreements with maturity, respect, and a commitment to finding win-win solutions? Or do you resort to low blows, silent treatments, or attempts to dominate or control your partner?

The difference often comes down to boundaries. When you're able to maintain healthy, loving boundaries even in the heat of an argument, you create the conditions for conflicts to be generative rather than destructive. You stay connected to your own truth without losing sight of your partner's humanity. You fight for your relationship, not against each other.

This isn't easy. When emotions run high and the stakes feel real, it's tempting to throw our boundaries out the window and go into full attack or defense mode. We might say things we later regret or shut down and withdraw in an attempt to protect ourselves.

For those of us with a history of trauma or unhealthy relationship patterns, conflict can be downright terrifying. It might trigger deep fears of abandonment, rejection, or even violence. These old wounds send us into fight, flight, or freeze mode before we even realize what's happening.

If this resonates with you, know that you're not alone. Most of us never learned how to "fight fair" or maintain our boundaries in the face of relational stress. We may have grown up in homes where conflict was explosive or completely avoided. We may have been punished for expressing anger or disappointment. We may have learned that conflict is dangerous and should be avoided at all costs.

But here's the truth: conflict itself is not the problem. When approached with skill and care, conflict can actually be an opportunity for growth, deepening understanding, and even greater intimacy. It's through the fires of honest disagreement that we learn to see each other more fully, stretch our empathy, and find creative solutions that work for both partners.

The key is learning to navigate conflict in a way that honors both your boundaries and your relationship. It's about developing the tools to stay grounded in your own truth while remaining open to your partner's experience. It's about fighting smart, not dirty.

This chapter will guide you through maintaining healthy boundaries even in the most challenging of conflicts. You'll learn how to identify your personal conflict style and triggers, communicate your needs and feelings with clarity and care, and repair the connection after a rupture. With practice (and a lot of self-compassion), you'll become a conflict ninja, handling relational storms with grace and strength.

• • • • ● ● • ● • ● • •

Identifying Your Conflict Style

Before diving into the nitty-gritty of boundary skills, take a moment to reflect on your relationship with conflict. We each have our own history, temperament, and triggers when it comes to disagreements. Understanding yours is a key first step in fighting smarter.

Consider these questions:

- How did your family of origin handle conflict? Was there a lot of yelling and door-slamming, or an eerie silence and avoidance? What messages did you internalize about anger and disagreement in relationships?

- What's your typical response when tensions rise with your partner? Do you tend to get loud and confrontational, or quiet and withdrawn? Do you try to smooth things over quickly or dig in your heels and stand your ground?

- What are your biggest fears when it comes to relational conflict? Abandonment? Rejection? Judgment? Loss of control? What core wounds or past traumas get activated in the heat of an argument?

- How do you typically feel in your body during a disagreement? Is there tightness in your chest, a sinking feeling in your stomach, or a hot flush of anger or shame? Where do you carry the stress and intensity of conflict?

- What helps you feel more grounded and centered during relational stress? Deep breaths? A quick walk around the block? A hand on your heart? What are your go-to self-regulation tools?

As you reflect, you might notice patterns in your conflict style. Maybe you're a "pursuer," chasing after your partner for connection and resolution. Or maybe you're a "withdrawer," pulling away when things get heated. You might have a "fight" response, getting aggressive to control the situation, or a "freeze" response, going quiet to avoid further escalation.

Whatever your style, there's no shame or blame here. It's simply a product of your unique wiring and experiences. The goal isn't to judge yourself but to bring compassionate curiosity to your patterns.

Understanding your conflict blueprint helps you make more conscious, boundaried choices. When you recognize your triggers and conflict habits, you're more likely to respond with intention rather than reactivity.

Self-awareness is key because let's be real—most of us are not our most skillful selves during a heated argument. When our blood is boiling and defenses are up, it's hard to remember all those healthy communication techniques we've read about. But by deepening your awareness, you build a foundation of resilience for those tough moments.

• • • • • • • • • •

Communicating Your Truth with Care

Now that you have a clearer understanding of your conflict style and triggers, it's time to learn how to communicate your needs, feelings, and perspectives in a way that honors both your truth and your relationship.

Here are some key principles to keep in mind:

1. Use "I" Statements.
Instead of saying, "You always..." or "You never...," try "I feel..." or "I need...". This keeps the focus on your own experience and avoids the blame and defensiveness that "you" statements can trigger.

2. Be Specific and Direct.
Avoid vague generalizations or beating around the bush. If you're feeling hurt by something your partner said, name it clearly: "When you made that joke about my job, I felt belittled." Clarity is kindness in conflict.

3. Make Space for Your Partner's Experience.
Expressing your truth doesn't mean invalidating your partner's. Use language that acknowledges multiple perspectives, like, "This is how I experienced that moment, and I'm curious to hear your take on it too."

4. Stay Anchored in the Present.

It's tempting to bring up past grievances during conflict, but that can quickly escalate things. Focus on the current issue and what you need to resolve it.

5. Remember the Goal: Connection and Understanding.

You're not trying to "win" the argument or prove your partner wrong. You're expressing your truth to be more fully seen and heard. The goal is mutual understanding.

6. Take Timeouts When Needed.

If things are getting too heated, it's okay to press pause. Say something like, "I'm feeling too triggered right now to have a productive conversation. Can we take a break and come back to this when we're calmer?"

These principles are simple in theory but difficult in practice, especially when emotions are high. It takes courage and vulnerability to communicate boundaries clearly, but with time and effort, you can learn to express even your most challenging truths with love.

· · · ● · ● · ● · ● · · ·

Boundary-Honoring Conflict in Action

Let's see what it looks like to fight with boundaries in a real-life scenario.

Imagine this situation: You've come home after a long, exhausting day at work. All you want is some quality time with your partner. But when you walk in, they're in the living room, deeply engrossed in a video game with their friends online. You feel hurt and neglected.

In an unboundaried state, you might:

- Sulk in the bedroom, giving your partner the cold shoulder and hoping they'll notice your displeasure.

- Storm into the living room and yell at your partner for being inconsiderate, demanding they drop everything to be with you.

- Pretend everything's fine while silently fuming and resenting your partner.

None of these reactions would serve you or your relationship. They involve emotional dishonesty, power struggles, and unmet expectations.

Now imagine approaching the situation with healthy boundaries:You take a deep breath, tuning into your emotions. Beneath the hurt and frustration, you realize you're feeling lonely and unimportant. You recognize you had an unmet expectation of quality time, which triggered your emotional response.

When your partner takes a break from gaming, you calmly express your truth:"Hey, I noticed I'm feeling a bit hurt and lonely tonight. I was hoping we'd spend some quality time together after work. When I saw you gaming instead, I felt unimportant. Could we talk about how we can balance our solo time and time together in the future?"

Notice how this **response:**

- Uses "I" statements to own your feelings.

- Names your unmet need clearly.

- Avoids blame and stays focused on the present moment.

- Opens the door for collaborative problem-solving.

This doesn't magically resolve the conflict, but it sets the stage for a respectful conversation. You're not attacking, withdrawing, or expecting your partner to read your mind. You're sharing vulnerably and inviting a conversation that strengthens connection.

Now let's look at a scenario where you're on the receiving end of a boundary during conflict.

Imagine you and your partner are arguing about household chores. In frustration, you blurt out, "Why am I always the one who has to do everything? You never help!"

Your partner takes a deep breath and responds with a boundary:"When you say I never help, I feel hurt and unappreciated. I'm also feeling overwhelmed by everything we have to manage. I need us to find a solution that works for both of us. Can we cool off for a bit and come back together to make a plan that feels fair?"

In this moment, your partner:

- Names their hurt and sets a boundary.

- Expresses their need for fairness and collaboration.

- Redirects the conversation toward connection.

Though it's not always easy to receive this type of communication in the heat of conflict, recognizing it as an act of boundary-setting can open the door to a healthier conversation.

Fighting with boundaries transforms conflict into an opportunity for deeper intimacy and growth. It allows both partners to express difficult emotions without resorting to harmful behaviors. And with each conflict navigated skillfully, the relationship becomes stronger.

· · · · ● · ● · ● · · ·

When Boundaries Break Down: Navigating Rupture and Repair

Even with the best intentions, sometimes boundaries break down. We say things we don't mean or fall back into unhealthy patterns. These moments can be deeply painful, filling us with shame and regret. But breakdowns aren't the end—they're part of the relational process. What matters most is how we repair after these ruptures.

If you find yourself in the midst of a boundary breakdown, here are steps you can take:

1. Press Pause and Self-Soothe.
First, get yourself into a calmer state. This isn't the time to fix things; it's the time to practice self-care.

2. Take Responsibility and Apologize.
Reflect on your actions and their impact. Own up to what you said or did, and express genuine remorse.

3. Give Your Partner Space.

Your partner may need time to process their feelings. Respect their need for space and don't push for immediate resolution.

4. Reflect and Get Curious.

What triggered the rupture? What unmet needs or wounds were at play? How could you handle a similar situation differently in the future?

5. Engage in Repair.

When you're both ready, come together to talk through the rupture. Be vulnerable, take responsibility, and explore how to prevent similar situations in the future.

Ruptures are not a sign that your relationship is doomed. With care and effort, they can be opportunities for healing and growth. What matters is your willingness to repair and reconnect.

Workbook Exercise: Conflict Debrief

Alright, boundary-builders! It's time to take your conflict skills from the theoretical to the practical. In this exercise, you'll have the opportunity to reflect on a recent disagreement with your partner and identify opportunities for more boundaried communication.

Think of it like a post-game analysis for your relationship. You'll be breaking down the play-by-play of your conflict, not to keep score or assign blame, but to extract the learning and growth opportunities.

So grab your boundary goggles and let's dive in!

Step 1: Choose Your Conflict

Think back to a recent disagreement or argument you had with your partner. It could be a minor spat or a major blowout—the key is that it's fresh in your memory and had some emotional charge for you.

As you reflect on the conflict, jot down a brief summary of:

1. What the disagreement was about (the topic or trigger)

2. How it started (who said what first)

3. What each of you did or said in the heat of the moment

4. How it ended or got resolved (if it did)

Try to stick to the facts here, without too much interpretation or judgement. The goal is simply to have a clear picture of the conflict to work with.

Step 2: Map Your Triggers

Now that you've got your conflict outlined, it's time to dive a little deeper into your own experience. Put on your emotional detective hat and see if you can identify:

1. What got triggered for you in this conflict? Was it a fear of abandonment, a sense of being controlled, a feeling of inadequacy? Try to name the core wound or vulnerability that got activated.

2. How did you know you were triggered? What sensations did you notice in your body (racing heart, tight chest, hot face)? What emotions came up for you (anger, sadness, shame)?

3. How did you react when you were triggered? Did you get loud and confrontational, or shut down and withdraw? Did you try to smooth things over, or dig in your heels?

4. What boundaries, if any, did you cross in your triggered state? Did you say something you later regretted, or did you stuff down your true feelings to keep the peace?

Remember, there's no shame in getting triggered. It's a normal, human part of being in relationship. The key is to bring mindful awareness to your patterns so you can start to shift them.

Step 3: Imagine a Boundaried Response

Now that you've got some clarity on your triggers and reactions, let's explore how you might approach the conflict differently with your boundary skills engaged.

Imagine rewinding the tape of your disagreement to the moment you first felt triggered. Now, press pause and consider:

1. What if, instead of reacting automatically, you took a deep breath and checked in with yourself? What if you gave yourself permission to feel your feelings, without judgement?

2. From this more grounded place, how might you express your truth with care? What "I statements" could you use to own your experience, without blame or accusation?

3. How might you make space for your partner's experience, too? What questions could you ask to better understand their perspective?

4. If things started to escalate, how might you press pause and ask for a timeout? What self-soothing tools could you use to regain your cool?

5. And if a boundary did get crossed (by you or your partner), how might you take responsibility and initiate repair? What would a heartfelt apology sound like?

Write out a sample script for how this boundaried version of the conflict might have unfolded. For example:

"When you said [hurtful comment], I noticed I felt flooded with shame and anger. I had the urge to lash out and say something equally hurtful. But I'm trying to practice expressing my truth with care. So here's what's true for me: [vulnerable share about your experience]. I imagine you have your own truth too, and I want to make space to hear it. Can we slow this down and have a real conversation about what we're both needing here?"

The point here is not to script a "perfect" response (spoiler alert: there isn't one!), but to start training your brain to reach for your boundary tools in the heat of the moment. With practice, this new way of relating will start to feel more natural.

Step 4: Share and Practice with Your Partner

If you feel comfortable, consider sharing your Conflict Debrief with your partner. You might invite them to do the exercise on their own first, and then come together to share your reflections and imagined re-dos.

As you share, remember: the goal is not to rehash the original conflict or prove who was "right" or "wrong." It's to practice vulnerability, empathy, and collaborative problem-solving.

Some tips for a productive sharing session:

- Take turns sharing, without interrupting or getting defensive. Practice deep listening and reflection ("What I hear you saying is...").

- Validate each other's experiences, even if you disagree. Acknowledging your partner's perspective doesn't mean abandoning your own truth.

- Look for the kernels of wisdom and growth in each other's shares. What new insights or understandings are emerging? What requests or boundaries feel important to honor moving forward?

- Celebrate your courage in showing up for this vulnerable work! Acknowledge that you're both learning and growing together, and that conflict is an opportunity for deeper intimacy.

If you want to take it a step further, consider role-playing your imagined boundary re-dos together. Take turns being the boundary-setter and the boundary-receiver, and practice embodying the skills of clear communication, empathetic listening, and collaborative repair.

Yes, it might feel a bit awkward or staged at first. That's okay! With repetition, these new ways of relating will start to become second nature. You're literally rewiring your brains for healthier, more connected conflict.

Step 5: Rinse and Repeat

Relationships are a life-long learning lab, and conflicts are some of our juiciest opportunities for growth. So don't just stop at one Conflict Debrief—make it a regular part of your relational hygiene!

After every disagreement (or at least the ones that feel significant), take some solo time to map your triggers, imagine a boundaried re-do, and extract the learning. Then, when you're both ready, come together to share your reflections and practice your skills.

Over time, you'll start to notice patterns and themes in your conflicts. You'll develop a shared language and toolbox for navigating tension. You'll find yourselves catching reactive cycles before they spiral, and repairing ruptures with more ease and speed. And most importantly, you'll experience the magic of using conflict to deepen intimacy, rather than destroy it. You'll discover that the "terrible twos" moments of relationships—the tantrums and meltdowns and messiness—are actually portals to profound growth and connection.

So keep showing up, even when it's hard. Keep turning towards each other, even when everything in you wants to bolt or attack. Keep believing in your capacity to fight for your love, one boundaried breath at a time.

Because that's the real work of intimacy: not avoiding conflicts, but learning to wade through them with grace, humility, and an unwavering commitment to your own and each other's growth.

THE TIME-OUT TRICK: HOW TO PRESS PAUSE WITHOUT HITTING REWIND ON THE FIGHT

Picture this: You and your partner are in the middle of a heated argument. Voices are raised, hearts are pounding, and your mind is racing with all the ways your partner is wrong. You're on a roll, ready to unleash your full arsenal of grievances when, suddenly, you remember something important—*you have the power to press pause.*

You don't have to keep riding this train to its inevitable crash. You can step off, take a breath, and find your way back to center. Welcome to the world of relational time-outs, an underrated yet invaluable tool in the boundary-setting toolkit.

Time-outs often get a bad rap in our culture. They're seen as a sign of weakness, as if you're avoiding the "real" issue. We've been conditioned to believe that "true love" means fighting it out until you reach a resolution, no matter how ugly or exhausting the process. But in reality, time-outs aren't about avoidance. They're about creating space for de-escalation, self-soothing, and returning to the conversation with clearer minds and more open hearts.

Think of a coach calling a time-out during a sports game. They don't do it because they're giving up; they do it to give their players a chance to regroup, breathe, and remember the game plan. Your relational time-outs serve the same purpose. They allow you to step out of reactive mode and reconnect with what truly matters—your relationship.

The magic of time-outs isn't just in de-escalating conflict. By learning to press pause in the midst of tension, you're rewiring your brain for healthier, more connected communication. Every time you choose to take a break rather than bulldoze through a fight, you're strengthening your ability to regulate emotions and return to calm. Over time, this becomes a kind of relational superpower. You develop the ability to stay centered, even in the face of your partner's intensity, and lead with love rather than reacting with anger.

But make no mistake—time-outs aren't a substitute for working through issues. They're a strategy for engaging with conflict in a healthier, more productive way. Think of them as training for your "wise warrior" self: You're not running from the battle; you're learning to choose your battles wisely and fight smarter, not harder.

In this chapter, we'll dive into how to effectively use time-outs during conflict. You'll learn how to recognize when it's time to take a break, how to communicate your need for space, and how to craft a game plan for making the most of your pause. Let's get started.

$$\bullet \; \bullet \; \bullet \; \bullet \; \bullet \; \bullet \; \bullet \; \bullet \; \bullet$$

Calling the Time-Out: When and How to Take a Break

Imagine you're in the middle of a tense conversation with your partner. Maybe it's about their offhand comment at dinner or the pile of dishes they've left in the sink for days. As you start to feel your frustration rise, your body gives you clear signals that things are escalating—your heart races, your palms sweat, and your thoughts narrow into a tunnel vision of righteous indignation.

This is your cue. This is when your boundary alarm should go off, signaling that it's time to take a break before the conflict escalates further. But how do you know when it's time for a time-out? Here are some common signs:

- **Physical signs**: Rapid heartbeat, shallow breathing, tense muscles, feeling flushed or hot.

- **Emotional signs**: Overwhelm, rage, panic, feeling shut down or numb.

- **Mental signs**: Black-and-white thinking, defensiveness, a lack of empathy for your partner's perspective.

- **Behavioral signs**: Raising your voice, getting sarcastic, stomping around, giving the silent treatment.

When you notice these signs in yourself (or your partner), it's time to call a time-out. This doesn't mean you're giving up or avoiding the issue. Instead, you're giving yourself and your partner the gift of a pause—an opportunity to regroup, calm down, and re-engage with more clarity and care.

How to Call a Time-Out

Here's how to effectively call a time-out during conflict:

- **Use "I" statements**: Own your experience and take responsibility for your need for a break. For example, say, "I'm feeling really overwhelmed right now and need some space to calm down."

- **Propose a specific time frame**: Suggest a time to reconvene and commit to coming back to the conversation. For instance, "Can we take a break for 20 minutes and then check back in?"

- **Affirm your commitment**: Reassure your partner that you're invested in the relationship and want to work through the issue together. "I care about us, and I want to come back to this when I can respond with more clarity."

What Not to Do During a Time-Out

While time-outs can be incredibly effective, there are some pitfalls to avoid:

- **Don't use a time-out to punish your partner**: Don't say, "I'm done dealing with you," and storm out. Time-outs should be about self-care, not manipulation.

- **Don't disappear**: Make sure your partner knows when you'll return to the conversation so they don't feel abandoned.

- **Don't stew**: The goal of a time-out isn't to sit in anger or rehearse your comebacks. Use the break to cool down and shift into a more open mindset.

If your partner resists your request for a time-out, explain that it's not about avoiding the issue but creating a better space to address it. You might say, "I'm not trying to run away from this conversation. I want to work through it, but I need a break to make sure I can respond in a way that's constructive."

If they continue to push back, it's okay to take a break anyway. Remember, you're responsible for your actions, not your partner's reactions. By respecting your own boundaries, you're modeling healthy behavior that can influence your partner over time.

• • • ● • ● • • • •

Crafting Your Time-Out Game Plan

You've successfully called a time-out and stepped away from the heat of the moment. Now what? How do you use this pause productively rather than stewing in frustration or rehearsing your next zinger?

A relational time-out isn't a passive break—it's an active practice. Your goal is to shift your state of mind and body so that you can return to the conversation with more calm, clarity, and openness.

Here's a sample time-out game plan to guide you:

1. **Separate and Self-Soothe**
   Find a space where you can be alone with your thoughts—another room, a walk outside, wherever you can breathe freely. Start by doing something that helps

calm your nervous system. This might be deep breathing, splashing cold water on your face, or listening to a calming song.

2. **Feel Your Feelings**

Allow yourself to feel the emotions that are coming up—anger, hurt, fear, or sadness. Don't judge or suppress your feelings, but don't let them control you either. You might want to journal to help process the emotions, getting them out on paper.

3. **Reality-Check Your Story**

Once you've calmed down a bit, take a step back and examine the story you're telling yourself. Are you painting your partner as the villain? Are you catastrophizing the situation? Try to poke holes in that narrative. Ask yourself, "What else could be true?"

4. **Reconnect with Your Values**

Take a moment to reflect on what really matters in this situation. What kind of partner do you want to be? What do you value most in your relationship? This will help you come back to the conversation with more focus on connection and resolution.

5. **Reach Out for Support**

If you need extra perspective, reach out to a trusted friend or therapist. Remember, the goal is to calm down and gain clarity—not to vent or vilify your partner. A good friend will help you reflect rather than fuel your anger.

Your time-out is an opportunity to shift from reactivity to responsiveness. When you're ready to return, you don't need to have all the answers. It's okay to come back with humility and curiosity.

• • ● • ● • ● • ● • • •

Re-Engaging with Care: Coming Back After a Break

You've taken your time-out and found your center. Now it's time to re-engage with your partner and dive back into the conversation with a fresh perspective. Here's how to do it:

1. Start with Appreciation and Vulnerability

Thank your partner for giving you the space you needed, and acknowledge that taking a break wasn't easy for either of you. Share a little of what came up for you during the time-out and be honest if you're still feeling tender or unsure.

Example: "Thank you for giving me the space to cool down. I realized I still have some strong feelings, but I want to approach this with an open heart and hear your side too."

2. Lead with Curiosity, Not Conviction

Re-enter the conversation with curiosity about your partner's experience. Ask open-ended questions and listen without interrupting. Focus on understanding their feelings rather than defending your position.

Example: "I'd love to hear more about how you were feeling earlier. What was going through your mind when we started arguing?"

3. Own Your Part

Take responsibility for anything you realized during the time-out, such as how you may have contributed to the conflict. Apologize sincerely if you crossed any boundaries.

Example: "During the break, I realized I interrupted you and got defensive, and I'm sorry. That wasn't fair to you, and I'll work on being more patient."

4. Collaborate on Solutions

Shift the conversation from blame to collaboration. Discuss ways you can both address the issue and brainstorm solutions that meet both your needs. Emphasize teamwork and mutual respect.

Example: "It seems like we're both feeling overwhelmed. How can we work together to make sure we're both feeling supported? What would help us both feel better?"

5. Celebrate the Small Wins

Even if the conversation is still unresolved, take a moment to acknowledge your progress. Celebrate the fact that you're both trying to engage with love and respect, and recognize the courage it takes to communicate honestly.

Example: "I really appreciate how we both stayed calm and open in this conversation. It makes me feel hopeful about how we handle things moving forward."

Re-engaging after a time-out is less about finding an immediate solution and more about creating a safe space for deeper understanding and connection. If the conversation needs more time, don't be afraid to take another break or continue the dialogue later.

Workbook Exercise: The Time-Out Plan

Alright, it's time to get practical and personal with your time-out skills! In this exercise, you'll create a customized Time-Out Plan for your relationship—a clear, agreed-upon protocol for how you'll press pause and reconnect in the midst of conflict.

Think of this as your relational first-aid kit. Just like you wouldn't wait until you're bleeding to figure out where the bandages are, you don't want to wait until you're in the heat of a fight to figure out your time-out strategy. By creating this plan proactively with your partner, you set yourselves up for more skillful, connected conflict navigation.

So grab your partner, your boundary wisdom, and your favorite planning tools (colorful pens highly encouraged), and let's get crafting!

Step 1: Reflect on Your Time-Out Needs and Patterns

Before you dive into creating your joint plan, take some solo time to reflect on your own relationship with time-outs. Grab your journal or a piece of paper and jot down your responses to the following prompts:

1. What are my personal signs that I'm getting escalated or flooded during a conflict? (e.g. racing heart, feeling trapped, lashing out with sarcasm)

2. What helps me calm down and re-center when I'm feeling triggered? (e.g. deep breaths, a splash of cold water, a quick walk outside)

3. What are my fears or concerns when it comes to taking time-outs? (e.g. that it means I'm weak, that my partner will think I don't care)

4. What do I need from my partner to feel safe and respected when one of us calls a time-out? (e.g. a clear commitment to return, an acknowledgment of my feelings)

5. What does my ideal post-time-out re-engagement look like? (e.g. leading with appreciation, owning my part, brainstorming solutions together)

As you reflect, try to be as specific and honest as possible. The more clarity you have about your own needs and patterns, the more effectively you can communicate them to your partner and co-create a plan that works for both of you.

Step 2: Share and Listen with Your Partner

Once you've both had a chance to reflect individually, come together to share your insights and listen deeply to each other's perspectives. Find a comfy spot where you can sit face-to-face without too many distractions (pro tip: phones on airplane mode).

Take turns sharing your responses to the reflection prompts above, using the following guidelines:

- Speak from your own experience using "I" statements (e.g. "I feel," "I need,"

"My concern is")

- Share one prompt at a time, and then pause to let your partner reflect back what they heard. This ensures you're really taking in each other's perspectives.

- Ask clarifying questions if something is unclear, but resist the urge to debate or defend. The goal here is understanding, not agreement.

- Validate each other's experiences, even if they differ from your own. A simple "that makes sense" or "I can see how that would be important to you" can go a long way.

- Make note of any common themes or areas of alignment. These will be helpful building blocks for your joint plan.

Remember, this conversation isn't about finding the "right" answers, but about getting curious about each other's inner worlds. The more you can approach it with openness and care, the more solid your time-out foundation will be.

Step 3: Craft Your Time-Out Plan

Now it's time to put your heads (and hearts) together and craft your customized Time-Out Plan! Using your individual reflections and shared insights as a guide, work together to create a written document that covers the following elements:

1. Time-Out Signals: How will you communicate that you need a time-out? This could be a verbal phrase (e.g. "I need a pause"), a physical gesture (e.g. hands in a T-shape), or even a silly code word that lightens the tension (e.g. "Pineapple!"). The key is to choose something you both feel comfortable with and can remember in the heat of the moment.

2. Time-Out Parameters: Get specific about the logistics of your time-outs.

   ○ How long will your default time-out period be? (e.g. 20 minutes, an hour)

   ○ Where will you physically go during a time-out? (e.g. separate rooms, a walk around the block)

○ Are there any ground rules for what's off-limits during a time-out? (e.g. no alcohol, no ranting to friends)

3. Solo Care Strategies: What will each of you do during your solo time-out to calm down and gain perspective? Refer back to your individual reflections for ideas, and get as specific as possible. For example:

○ "I will do a 5-minute guided breathing meditation using my favorite app."

○ "I will journal using the prompt 'What do I really want in this situation?'"

○ "I will take a short walk and focus on noticing the colours and sounds around me."

4. Re-Engagement Protocol: How will you reconnect and re-enter the conversation after a time-out? Again, get specific about what this will look and sound like. For example:

○ "We will meet back in the living room at the agreed-upon time."

○ "Whoever called the time-out will initiate with an appreciation for the other's willingness to pause."

○ "We will each share one insight or shift that emerged during our solo time, using 'I' statements."

○ "We will brainstorm at least 3 possible win-win solutions before settling on a course of action."

5. Back-Up Support: Despite our best intentions, there may be times when your solo strategies aren't enough to fully de-escalate. Decide together on some "lifelines" you can call on if you need extra support.

○ Do you have any trusted friends, family members, or professionals who can offer guidance or perspective?

○ Are there any resources (books, articles, workshops) that you find helpful for navigating conflict?

  ○ How will you communicate if you need to call in outside support, and what parameters will you set around confidentiality?

As you craft your plan, remember: The goal isn't to create rigid rules, but to establish a flexible framework that honors both of your needs and supports your relational resilience. If something doesn't feel quite right, keep tweaking until you land on a version that feels good to both of you.

Step 4: Road-Test and Revise

Congratulations, you've created your Time-Out Plan! But remember, like any good first-aid kit, it's meant to be used, not just admired. So the next time you find yourselves in a conflict, pull out your plan and put it into action.

After you've had a chance to use your plan a few times, come back together and debrief on how it's working. Consider questions like:

• What parts of our Time-Out Plan felt most helpful or effective?

• Were there any moments when our plan broke down or didn't quite fit the situation? What can we learn from those?

• Are there any elements we want to add, remove, or modify based on our real-life experience?

• How do we feel our time-out practice is impacting our overall conflict navigation and relational resilience?

Based on your reflections, make any adjustments to your plan that feel necessary. Remember, your Time-Out Plan is a living document—it's meant to evolve with you as you grow and learn together.

So be patient with yourselves and each other as you find your time-out groove.

Celebrate the moments of success, and get curious about the moments of struggle.

And above all, keep coming back to the spirit of care and collaboration that inspired this practice in the first place.

With every time-out you navigate together, you're not just pressing pause on a fight. You're strengthening your muscles of love, one boundaried breath at a time.

You're reminding yourselves that your relationship is more precious than any single problem. You're choosing the brave path of intimacy again and again.

PART VI: BUILDING TRUST WITH BOUNDARIES: THE ROAD TO REPAIR

CHAPTER ELEVEN

TRUST REPAIR 101: HOW BOUNDARIES HELP HEAL BROKEN BONDS

In the dance of intimate relationships, trust is the invisible thread that holds everything together. It allows us to soften into vulnerability, take emotional risks, and surrender to the beautiful uncertainty of loving and being loved. But what happens when that thread gets frayed—or even severed? When a boundary violation, betrayal, or an accumulation of hurts erodes the foundation of safety and security? Suddenly, the dance floor becomes a minefield, each step tentative, each twirl tinged with trepidation.

If you've experienced a rupture of trust, you know how destabilizing and disorienting it can be. It leaves you questioning everything: Can I ever trust them again? Will I ever feel safe letting my guard down? Am I foolish for even wanting to try?

First, know that I see you. It takes courage to sit with these questions and confront the shattered pieces of something once sacred. And while it might feel impossible right now, healing is possible. Repair is possible. Trust, once broken, can be rebuilt—not in spite of the breach, but because of how you and your partner navigate it together.

This is where boundaries become essential. Healthy boundaries—clear, consistent, and mutually respectful—are critical to trust repair. They create a scaffolding of safety within which the delicate work of relational restoration can take place.

Trust is more than a cognitive calculation. It's a visceral feeling of safety that, once ruptured, activates our fear centers. We're suddenly hypervigilant, scanning for further betrayal, and operating from a place of self-protection. Boundaries offer a balm for the nervous system, restoring predictability and safety. They communicate reliability, reaffirm respect, and provide the foundation for rebuilding trust.

In this chapter, we'll explore:

1. The neurobiology of trust and how boundaries help soothe the stress response.

2. Common trust-rupturing behaviors and how to address them with boundary-setting.

3. A step-by-step process for rebuilding trust after a boundary violation.

4. Practices for self-trust and self-compassion during relational uncertainty.

5. Real-life stories of couples who have used boundaries to heal and strengthen their connection.

Take a deep breath and summon your courage. Trust repair is not for the faint of heart, but it is for the openhearted. And that, dear one, is you.

· · · ● · ● · ● ● · ·

The Neurobiology of Trust and Boundaries

Trust, from a neurobiological perspective, is rooted in predictability. Our brains are wired to scan the environment for safety and threat, constantly trying to predict what will happen next. In a trusting relationship, our nervous system relaxes, knowing it can count on a certain level of stability and attunement from the other person. This allows us to feel safe—a "secure base" from which to explore the world.

When trust is ruptured, the brain's fear center, the amygdala, kicks into overdrive. Hypervigilance takes over, and our stress hormone levels spike, preparing us for fight, flight, or freeze. We become locked in a state of high alert, making it difficult to think clearly or engage productively with the situation at hand.

This is where boundaries come into play. Boundaries reintroduce predictability into the relationship, reassuring the nervous system that, even amid uncertainty, there are clear and reliable lines that will be respected. When someone who violated trust agrees to specific boundaries and follows through with consistency, it sends a powerful message to the brain: "You can trust me again. I will honor these commitments."

Repeated acts of boundary-keeping slowly begin to rebuild trust. It's a gradual process that involves rewiring the brain to associate the person with safety and reliability once more. This is why boundaries are not just about the external conditions of the relationship; they also help the brain relearn how to trust.

Common Trust-Rupturing Behaviors and Boundary Responses

Let's talk about some common trust-rupturing behaviors and how to address them with boundaries.

1. Lying and Deception

Whether it's small fibs or major betrayals, lying shatters trust. It creates a sense of unpredictability and makes the betrayed partner question what else might be hidden.

Boundary Response: "I need honesty in our relationship. Even small lies make me question what else might be untrue. If it happens again, I'll need space to reevaluate our relationship."

2. Breaking Agreements

Trust is built on keeping promises, no matter how small. When promises are broken, it erodes confidence in the other person's reliability.

Boundary Response: "When you break our agreements, like coming home later than you said without communicating, I feel disrespected. I need to be able to count on you to follow through on your word, or at least let me know when something comes up."

3. Emotional Invalidation

When feelings are dismissed or minimized, it creates emotional disconnection and insecurity. Trust is shaken when one partner feels unheard or misunderstood.

Boundary Response: "When you tell me I'm overreacting or being too sensitive, it shuts me down emotionally. I need my feelings to be acknowledged, even if you don't fully understand them."

4. Privacy Violations

Trust can be breached when private matters are shared without consent, or when personal boundaries around privacy (e.g., phones, journals) are violated.

Boundary Response: "When you shared my private story with others, it felt like a betrayal. I need you to respect my privacy and ask before sharing personal information about me or our relationship."

5. Inconsistent Availability

When one partner is emotionally or physically inconsistent, it creates insecurity in the relationship. Trust suffers when the other person can't be relied upon.

Boundary Response: "I need more consistency in your availability. When you cancel last minute or go quiet for days, it makes me feel unimportant. If this doesn't change, I'll need to make plans to support myself."

Each of these examples demonstrates how boundaries are not about punishment but about setting clear expectations for both partners moving forward.

• • • • ● • ● • ● • • •

A Step-by-Step Process for Rebuilding Trust After a Boundary Violation

Now that we've discussed the theory behind trust repair, let's dive into the practical steps. This is a roadmap to help you and your partner begin the journey of rebuilding trust.

1. Take Space to Regroup

Before jumping into repair, both partners should take time apart to reflect on what they need. Use this time to soothe your nervous system and process your emotions. Ask yourself: What do I need to feel safe again? What specific behaviors or commitments are necessary to rebuild trust?

2. Have a Boundary-Setting Conversation

Once you've both had space, sit down and have an open conversation. Use "I" statements to express how the trust violation impacted you and what boundaries are needed going forward. Make space for your partner's perspective as well.

3. Co-Create a Trust Repair Plan

Together, create a plan for repairing trust. This might include specific actions like increased communication, attending therapy, or checking in more frequently. Write it down so both partners are clear on expectations.

4. Take Small, Consistent Steps

Rebuilding trust isn't about grand gestures; it's about small, consistent actions over time. Celebrate each follow-through as a victory. For example, if the agreed-upon plan involves checking in after work every day, celebrate that effort.

5. Practice Patience and Self-Compassion

Rebuilding trust is a long, non-linear process. There will be setbacks. Practice patience and self-compassion, both with yourself and your partner. Trust that healing takes time.

6. Keep Coming Back to Your Boundaries

As you rebuild trust, stay vigilant about your boundaries. If old patterns resurface, address them quickly. Your boundaries are the foundation of the healing process.

· · · ● · ● · ● · ·

Practices for Self-Trust and Self-Compassion

Rebuilding trust isn't just about the relationship; it's also about rebuilding trust with yourself. When trust is broken, our faith in our own judgment often takes a hit. We may question our worth, intuition, or ability to trust again.

Here are some practices to help cultivate self-trust and self-compassion during this challenging time:

- **Mindful Self-Talk**: Speak to yourself as you would a close friend. Instead of criticizing yourself, offer kindness and validation.

- **Boundary Check-Ins**: Regularly ask yourself what boundaries you need to feel safe and respected.

- **Self-Care Rituals**: Create daily rituals that nurture your body and mind, like journaling or mindful breathing.

- **Embracing Vulnerability**: Stay open, even when it feels risky. Share your feelings with trusted friends or a therapist.

- **Forgiveness and Letting Go**: Forgive yourself for any perceived mistakes or failures. Trust that you're learning and growing through this experience.

· · · ● · ● · ● · · ·

Stories of Couples Who Have Rebuilt Trust

Real-life stories of couples who have successfully rebuilt trust can be a powerful source of inspiration and hope. Here are a few examples:

Sarah and Alex

Sarah and Alex had been together for ten years when Sarah discovered that Alex had been having an affair with a coworker. She was devastated, angry, and unsure if she could ever trust Alex again.

For months, they navigated the rocky terrain of betrayal and repair. Alex took full responsibility for his actions, committing to individual therapy to understand the roots of his infidelity. Sarah set clear boundaries around transparency and accountability moving forward.

Together, they attended couples therapy weekly, learning to communicate their needs and fears more vulnerably. They scheduled regular check-in dates to reconnect and attune to each other.

Slowly, painstakingly, they began to rebuild a foundation of trust and intimacy. It wasn't the same relationship they had before, but in many ways, it was deeper and more honest.

As Sarah reflects, "I never thought I would be grateful for the affair, but in a strange way, I am. It shattered the illusion that we had a perfect relationship and forced us to confront the parts of ourselves and each other that we'd been avoiding. It was incredibly painful, but it also led to a level of closeness and authenticity that we never had before."

Javier and Michael

Javier and Michael's trust rupture came in the form of broken agreements and inconsistent follow-through. For years, Michael struggled with alcohol abuse, often promising to cut back or seek help but ultimately falling back into old patterns.

Javier reached his breaking point when Michael got a DUI, putting both of their safety at risk. He set a firm boundary: "I love you, and I want to support your healing. But I can't be in a relationship where I'm constantly worrying if you're going to make it home alive. If you're not willing to get serious help for your drinking, I'll need to take some space and reevaluate our future together."

It was a wakeup call for Michael. With Javier's support and accountability, he entered a 90-day rehab program and began attending AA meetings regularly. He committed to rebuilding trust through consistent actions, not just words.

Javier and Michael also worked with a couples counselor to address the underlying issues that had contributed to Michael's drinking, like unresolved trauma and poor communication skills. They learned to set boundaries with love and to lean on each other in moments of vulnerability.

As Michael shares, "Getting sober was the hardest thing I've ever done, but it was also the most important. It not only saved my life, but it saved my relationship. Learning to show up for Javier consistently, to be a man of my word, has transformed every area of my life. I'm so grateful for his boundaries and his belief in my ability to change."

Lisa and Emily

Lisa and Emily's trust was ruptured through a series of small betrayals and emotional disconnections. Lisa had a habit of sharing intimate details of their relationship with her family and friends, despite Emily's requests for privacy. Emily often dismissed or minimized Lisa's feelings, leaving her feeling unheard and misunderstood.

The turning point came when Emily shared a deeply vulnerable story from Lisa's past in front of a group of acquaintances. Lisa was mortified and hurt, and the incident brought to light the many ways their trust had eroded over time.

They decided to take a three-month break from their relationship to reflect on what they really needed and wanted from each other. During that time, Lisa worked with a therapist to set stronger boundaries with her family and to practice more direct communication. Emily did her own work around emotional attunement and validation.

When they came back together, they were able to have more honest and compassionate conversations about their needs and fears. They created a relationship agreement that included specific boundaries around privacy, communication, and emotional safety.

As Lisa reflects, "Taking that break was scary, but it was also necessary. We needed to step back and really look at the patterns that were hurting our relationship. Learning to set boundaries was hard for me, but it ultimately allowed me to show up more fully and authentically with Emily. And feeling truly heard and understood by her has been a game-changer."

These stories illustrate that trust repair is possible, even in the face of deep betrayal. Each couple found their own way through, learning to use boundaries as tools for healing and connection.

Workbook Exercise: Trust Building Blueprint

Rebuilding trust after a boundary violation is a tender and courageous process, one that requires patience, commitment, and a clear roadmap for repair. In this exercise, you'll have the opportunity to create your own personalized Trust Building Blueprint—a step-by-step plan for restoring safety, accountability, and connection in your relationship.

Think of this blueprint as a collaborative construction project. You and your partner are the architects, designing a new foundation of trust from the ground up. You're taking the rubble of the betrayal and using it to build something stronger, sturdier, and more beautiful than before.

This process will require hard work, honest communication, and a willingness to confront uncomfortable truths. But it will also invite you into a deeper intimacy and understanding than you've ever known.

So roll up your sleeves, put on your hard hats, and let's get building!

Step 1: Reflect and Regroup

Before you start drafting your blueprint, take some time individually to reflect on the trust violation and its impact on you. Find a quiet, private space and journal your responses to the following prompts:

1. What specific boundary was crossed in this betrayal? What agreements or expectations were broken?

2. How did you feel in the immediate aftermath of discovering the betrayal? What emotions and physical sensations arose for you?

3. What has been the hardest part of coping with this breach of trust? What fears, doubts, or insecurities has it triggered?

4. What do you need to feel safe and secure in the relationship again? What specific actions or changes would help rebuild your trust?

5. In what ways have you been impacted by this betrayal? How has it affected your sense of self, your other relationships, your daily life?

Allow yourself to write freely and honestly, without censoring or judging your responses. If intense emotions arise, take breaks as needed, and consider reaching out for support from a trusted friend, family member, or therapist.

The goal of this reflection is not to dwell in the pain of the betrayal, but to gain clarity and self-understanding. The more you can name and validate your own experience, the better equipped you'll be to communicate your needs and boundaries in the repair process.

Step 2: Assess for Safety

Before moving into collaborative repair work, it's crucial to assess whether there is a sufficient foundation of physical and emotional safety in the relationship. If there are ongoing patterns of abuse, addiction, or uncontrolled mental health issues, rebuilding trust may not be possible or advisable without professional intervention. Take an honest look at your relationship and consider the following questions:

1. Is there a history of physical, sexual, or severe emotional abuse in the relationship?

2. Does my partner take full responsibility for their actions, or do they minimize, deny, or blame-shift when confronted with their behavior?

3. Is my partner willing and able to follow through on agreements and commitments, or do they consistently break their word?

4. Do I feel safe and respected when expressing my thoughts, feelings, and needs, or do I fear retaliation or rejection?

5. Is my partner open to seeking professional help and support (e.g. individual therapy, couples counseling, addiction recovery), or are they resistant to outside intervention?

If you answer yes to questions 1-4, or no to question 5, it's important to prioritize your own safety and well-being above repairing the relationship. Consult with a therapist or domestic violence advocate to create a safety plan and explore your options for support and protection.

Remember, you are not responsible for your partner's abusive or untrustworthy behavior, and you deserve to be treated with respect and care in all of your relationships.

Step 3: Set the Stage for Collaborative Repair

Once you've determined that there is a safe and willing foundation for repair work, it's time to come together with your partner to lay the groundwork for your trust building blueprint.

Set aside a focused block of time to have this conversation, and choose a location where you both feel comfortable and free from distractions. You may want to invite a therapist or mediator to facilitate the discussion if you anticipate it being particularly challenging or triggering.

Begin by setting some intentions and agreements for the conversation, such as:

- We will take turns speaking and listening without interruption

- We will use "I" statements to express our own thoughts and feelings

- We will seek to understand each other's perspectives, even if we disagree

- We will take breaks if the conversation starts to feel overwhelming or unproductive

- We will approach this as a team, committed to finding solutions that work for both of us

Once you've established these guidelines, take turns sharing your reflections from Step 1. Really listen to understand your partner's experience, resisting the urge to defend or explain. Practice validating each other's feelings, even if they're difficult to hear.

Then, move into a collaborative brainstorming session around what steps you each need to take to start rebuilding trust. Consider questions like:

- What specific boundaries need to be set or reinforced moving forward?

- What actions can the betraying partner take to demonstrate trustworthiness and accountability?

- What support does the betrayed partner need to feel safe and secure in the relationship again?

- How will you handle setbacks or slips in the future? What accountability and repair measures will you put in place?

Write down your ideas and commitments, getting as specific and concrete as possible. Remember, this is not about agreeing on a perfect solution, but about creating a living document that you can continue to refine and adapt as you move through the repair process.

Step 4: Create Your Trust Building Blueprint

With the groundwork laid, it's time to put pen to paper and draft your official Trust Building Blueprint. This document will serve as your roadmap for repair, outlining the specific steps you'll take to rebuild safety, accountability, and connection in your relationship.

Your blueprint will be unique to your situation, but here are some key elements to consider including:

1. **Boundary Agreements**: Clearly state the specific boundaries that need to be honored moving forward, such as:

   - "We agree to full transparency around cell phones, email accounts, and social media."

   - "We agree to a zero-tolerance policy for lying or deception, even about small things."

   - "We agree to set aside dedicated quality time together, free from distractions, at least once a week."

2. **Accountability Measures**: Outline how the betraying partner will take responsibility and demonstrate trustworthiness over time, such as:

   - Attending individual therapy to address underlying issues and patterns

   - Checking in with the betrayed partner on a daily basis to rebuild connection

   - Following through on agreed-upon actions and commitments consistently

   - Engaging in regular disclosure or polygraph testing (if infidelity was involved)

3. **Support for the Betrayed Partner**: Identify what the betrayed partner needs to feel safe, validated, and cared for in the aftermath of the betrayal, such as:

   - Attending individual therapy or support groups to process the trauma

   - Receiving regular reassurance and affection from the betraying partner

   - Having space and permission to express difficult emotions without judgment

- Taking time for self-care and healing activities, such as journaling or time in nature

4. **Relapse Prevention Plan**: Acknowledge that setbacks and slips may happen, and create a plan for how you'll handle them as a team, such as:

  - Agreeing to disclose any slips or temptations immediately, before they escalate

  - Scheduling extra therapy sessions or check-ins during high-risk times

  - Identifying triggers or stressors that could lead to a relapse, and creating coping strategies

  - Reinforcing boundaries and commitments, and adjusting the blueprint as needed

5. **Reconnection Rituals**: Brainstorm ways to actively rebuild intimacy, trust, and connection in your relationship, beyond just repairing the damage of the betrayal, such as:

  - Scheduling regular date nights or getaways to focus on having fun together

  - Practicing daily expressions of appreciation and admiration

  - Engaging in new hobbies or adventures that challenge you to grow together

  - Attending a couples retreat or workshop to deepen your communication and bond

As you create your blueprint, make sure each partner's needs and perspectives are well-represented. This should be a co-created document, not a list of demands from either side.

Once you have a draft you both feel good about, commit to following through on your agreements with consistency and integrity. Sign the document as a symbol of your dedication to the repair process.

Step 5: Review, Revise, and Recommit

Rebuilding trust is not a one-and-done event, but an ongoing journey of growth and healing. As such, your Trust Building Blueprint is meant to be a living, breathing document—one that evolves along with you and your relationship.

Make a plan to review your blueprint together on a regular basis, such as once a month or quarter. During these check-ins, reflect on questions like:

- How well are we following through on our agreements and commitments?

- What's working well in our repair process? What positive changes have we noticed?

- What's been challenging or triggering for each of us? Where do we need extra support?

- Are there any boundaries, rituals, or action steps we need to add, remove, or modify based on our current needs and situation?

Be honest about your progress and setbacks, and approach each check-in with openness, compassion, and a commitment to continuous improvement. Celebrate your wins, learn from your mistakes, and keep coming back to the blueprint as your anchor and guide.

Over time, as trust is rebuilt and your relationship is restored, you may find that you need the blueprint less and less. The agreements and habits you've created will naturally integrate into your daily life, becoming the new foundation on which your love story unfolds.

But even then, keep your blueprint in a special place, and revisit it from time to time. Let it be a reminder of the work you've done, the challenges you've overcome, the love you've chosen over and over again.

And if you find yourselves in a difficult or disconnected place in the future, return to the blueprint with fresh eyes. Let it guide you back to the basics of trust, respect, and care. Let it remind you of what you're fighting for, and who you're becoming together.

Closing Reflection

As we close this Trust Building Blueprint exercise, take a moment to honor yourself and your partner for the courage, vulnerability, and commitment you're bringing to this process. Rebuilding trust after a betrayal is one of the most challenging and brave undertakings a relationship can face.

By engaging in this work, you're not just healing your own hearts—you're strengthening the fabric of all your connections, present and future. You're becoming a model of resilience, renewal, and unconditional love.

CHAPTER TWELVE

THE GRATITUDE LOOP: HOW BOUNDARIES, APPRECIATION, AND RESPECT FEED EACH OTHER

As we come to the end of our boundary-setting journey together, I want to leave you with a vision. A vision of what's possible when we make honoring our own and each other's boundaries a daily, lifelong practice. A vision of the ripple effects, both subtle and seismic, that a boundary-full life can create.

Imagine, for a moment, a world where everyone took responsibility for their own needs and desires. Where we communicated our limits and expectations clearly and kindly, without guilt or apology. Where we respected each other's "no" as much as we celebrated each other's "yes."

In this world, relationships would be defined by true mutuality and interdependence. We would support each other's growth and self-actualization, rather than trying to control or change each other. We would approach conflicts and differences with curiosity and collaboration, rather than defensiveness and blame.

But this boundary-full world would not just transform our intimate partnerships. It would transform our relationship to ourselves, to our work, to our communities, and to the planet as a whole.

Imagine showing up to your job with a clear sense of your capacities and priorities. Saying "no" to projects that don't align with your values, and "yes" to opportunities that light you up. Setting healthy limits around your time and energy, and trusting your colleagues to do the same. Collaborating from a place of shared purpose and mutual respect, rather than competition and burnout.

Imagine parenting your children with a commitment to their autonomy and individuation. Giving them age-appropriate choices and responsibilities, and respecting their right to say "no" (even when it's inconvenient). Modeling self-care and self-assertion, and encouraging them to listen to their own inner guidance. Raising a generation of empowered, emotionally intelligent boundary-setters.

Imagine engaging with your extended family and friends from a place of choicefulness and authenticity. Participating in traditions and gatherings that nourish you, and opting out of those that drain you. Having honest conversations about your differences and needs, and finding creative ways to connect that honor everyone's boundaries. Building a chosen family of cherished, reciprocal relationships.

Imagine moving through the world with a deep reverence for your own and others' sovereignty. Asking for consent before touching someone or entering their space. Respecting the bodily autonomy and self-determination of people of all genders, races, abilities, and ages. Honoring the boundaries and sacred sites of indigenous lands and cultures. Treating the earth's resources as precious gifts to steward, not exploit.

This is the world that is possible when we embody our boundaries with consistency and care. A world of greater freedom, authenticity, and interconnection. A world where "no" is not a dirty word, but a holy one. A world where we honor our yeses and our nos in equal measure, trusting that therein lies the path to true intimacy and aliveness.

Of course, this boundary-full world is not some far-off utopia. It's a reality that we can start co-creating, right here, right now, in our own lives and relationships. With every limit we set and uphold, every "no" we speak and respect, every "yes" we offer from a place of full-hearted freedom—we are planting seeds of a more boundaried world.

And the amazing thing is, as we practice honoring our own and each other's boundaries, we start to experience a powerful positive feedback loop. A self-reinforcing cycle of appreciation, respect, and trust that makes setting and sustaining our boundaries easier and more natural over time.

I call this the Gratitude Loop, and here's how it works:

• • • ● • ● • ● •

The Gratitude Loop: A Positive Spiral of Boundary-Setting and Appreciation

When we first start setting boundaries in a relationship, it can feel awkward, even scary. We might worry about how the other person will react, or if we're doing it "right." We might feel guilty or selfish for asserting our needs, or fear that we'll be rejected or abandoned as a result.

But as we practice expressing our limits and expectations clearly and kindly, something miraculous starts to happen. The very act of setting a boundary becomes an invitation for greater connection and understanding.

Think about it: When you tell your partner, "I need some alone time to recharge tonight," you're not just asserting your need for solitude. You're also giving them a precious window into your inner world. You're sharing a vulnerable truth about what you need to feel balanced and whole.

And when your partner responds with respect and understanding—"I hear you. Take all the time you need. I'll be here when you're ready to connect again"—they are sending you a powerful message of love and acceptance. They are saying, in essence, "I see your needs as valid and important. I am willing to adjust my own desires to make space for yours."

This exchange of boundary-setting and respectful response creates a spark of appreciation. You feel seen, heard, and valued for your authentic self. Your partner feels trusted and appreciated for their flexibility and care.

And here's where the magic happens: The more appreciated and respected we feel for setting boundaries, the more motivated we are to keep setting them. And the more we keep setting them, the more appreciation and respect we generate in our relationships.

It's a positive spiral of boundary-setting and gratitude, each reinforcing the other. The more we practice honoring our own and each other's boundaries, the easier and more natural it becomes. We start to internalize the belief that our needs and limits are not just valid, but valuable. We start to trust that asserting our boundaries is not a threat to our relationships, but a pathway to deeper intimacy and connection.

And as we keep spinning in this Gratitude Loop, our boundaries start to become more than just a tool for self-protection. They become a way of expressing our deepest values and desires. A way of inviting others to know and love us more fully. A way of co-creating relationships and communities built on a foundation of mutual care, respect, and appreciation.

· · · · ● · ● · · ·

The Ripple Effects of a Boundary-Full Life

When we commit to a consistent boundary practice, infused with an attitude of gratitude, the positive effects ripple out far beyond our individual relationships. Here are just a few of the ways that living a boundary-full life can create healing and transformation on a larger scale:

1. We model healthy relating for others. When we embody clear, compassionate boundaries in our own relationships, we become a living example for those around us. Our children, friends, colleagues, and community members witness what it looks like to honor one's own and others' needs with respect and care. We plant seeds of possibility for more boundaried ways of being and relating.

2. We uplift marginalized voices and experiences. Boundaries are not just a personal practice, but a political one. When we assert our right to say "no" to oppressive systems and expectations, we create space for others to do the same. When we

respect the boundaries and bodily autonomy of people of all identities and abilities, we help build a world of greater safety, dignity, and justice for all.

3. We challenge toxic cultural norms. So much of our mainstream culture is built on the violation of personal and collective boundaries. From non-consensual touching to the exploitation of natural resources, from the glorification of overwork to the silencing of dissent—toxic boundary-crossing is embedded in many of our social norms and structures. As we practice living a boundary-full life, we start to question and resist these norms. We become a countercultural force for consent, sustainability, and interdependence.

4. We create more space for joy and aliveness. Boundaries are not just about preventing violation and harm. They are also about making space for the things that bring us the most joy, meaning, and fulfillment. When we learn to say "no" to the things that deplete us, we free up more energy and resources to say "yes" to the things that enliven us. We create more room for pleasure, creativity, adventure, and connection in our lives and in the world.

5. We cultivate greater resilience and adaptability. Life is full of challenges and changes, from personal losses to global crises. A consistent boundary practice helps us weather these storms with greater resilience and grace. When we know how to assert our needs and limits, how to respect others' differences and autonomy, how to find the balance between independence and interdependence—we become more adaptable and resourceful in the face of adversity. We learn to stay rooted in our own truth while also staying open to new possibilities and perspectives.

These are just a few of the ways that a boundary-full life ripples out to create a better world for all of us. And the beautiful thing is, we don't have to wait for these positive effects to trickle down from some grand social transformation. We can start experiencing them right now, in the microcosm of our own lives and relationships.

Every time we set and uphold a boundary with care, we are strengthening our own resilience and modeling a more compassionate way of being. Every time we appreciate someone else for honoring our limits, we are reinforcing the value of mutual respect and consent. Every time we make a choice that aligns with our deepest needs and values, we are contributing to a world of greater authenticity and aliveness.

$$\bullet \cdot \bullet \cdot \bullet \bullet \cdot \bullet \cdot \bullet \cdot \bullet \cdot \bullet$$

Living Your Boundary-Full Truth

As we come to the end of our journey together, I want to leave you with one final invitation. An invitation to keep living your boundary-full truth, one brave and imperfect day at a time.

Setting and maintaining healthy boundaries is a lifelong practice, not a one-time achievement. Even with all the tools and insights you've gained from this book, there will still be moments when you falter, when you say "yes" when you mean "no," or "no" when you mean "yes." There will be times when you over-accommodate others' needs at the expense of your own, or when you assert your limits with more harshness than heart.

This is all part of the messy, beautiful process of boundary-setting. The goal is not perfection, but presence. Not flawlessness, but flexibility. Not getting it right every time, but recommitting to your boundary practice with compassion and curiosity, again and again.

So as you go forth from these pages, remember that your worth is not measured by how perfectly you set your boundaries, but by how honestly you live your truth. Trust that your needs and desires are valid, simply because they are yours. Know that every time you assert your boundaries with care, you are not only honoring your own sacred "yes" and "no," but you are inviting others to do the same.

Keep spinning in the gratitude loop, appreciating yourself and others for the brave boundary work you are doing. Keep looking for opportunities to model and uplift a more boundaried way of being in all your circles of influence. Keep saying "yes" to the things that bring you alive, and "no" to the things that diminish your light.

And on those inevitable days when boundary-setting feels hard—when you're worried about disappointing someone, or when your "no" is met with resistance—come back to your breath. Come back to your body. Come back to the bedrock truth of your own inherent worthiness.

Remember that your boundaries are not a burden, but a blessing. A sacred responsibility to honor your own and others' sovereignty. A revolutionary act of love in a world that so often tells us to shrink, to hide, to betray ourselves for the sake of belonging.

But here's the liberating truth: You already belong. You belong to yourself, first and foremost. You belong to the vast web of interdependence that links us all. You belong to the unfolding story of healing and awakening that is calling us to live more boundaried lives, for our own sake and for the sake of the world.

Your boundary-full voice is needed, now more than ever. Your empowered "yes" and your compassionate "no" are threads in the tapestry of transformation that we are weaving together.

So keep showing up, dear one. Keep shining your light. Keep honoring your sacred boundaries, with devotion and with delight.

And know that with every courageous choice you make, you are co-creating a world where all of us can thrive—boundaried and beloved, sovereign and surrendered, gloriously free and utterly connected.

Workbook Exercise: Boundary Tune-Up Checklist

Congratulations! You've arrived at the end of our boundary-setting journey together. Take a moment to pause and honor yourself for all the brave and beautiful work you've done.

Over the course of these pages, you've explored the what, why, and how of creating healthy boundaries in your relationships and in your life. You've identified your core needs and desires, practiced asserting your limits with clarity and compassion, and learned to navigate boundary challenges with creativity and resilience.

Most importantly, you've begun to internalize the truth of your own inherent worth and wisdom. You've started to trust that your "yes" and your "no" are sacred gifts, not just for yourself, but for everyone whose life you touch.

Now, as we prepare to close this chapter and open the next, let's take some time to reflect on your key learnings, growth edges, and commitments moving forward. Think of this exercise as a loving boundary tune-up—a chance to celebrate your progress, clarify your intentions, and chart your course for the road ahead.

So find a quiet, comfy spot, grab your favorite journaling tools, and let's dive in!

Part 1: Celebrating Your Boundary Victories

Start by taking a few deep breaths and settling into a space of self-appreciation. Spend a few moments reflecting on your boundary journey so far, and then write down your responses to the following prompts:

1. What boundary skills or insights have you gained from this book that you're most proud of? What new tools are in your boundary toolkit?

2. Think of a recent situation where you set a boundary with more clarity, confidence, or compassion than you would have before. What did you do differently? How did it feel in your mind, body, and heart?

3. How have your relationships (with yourself and others) shifted or deepened as a result of your boundary work? What positive ripple effects are you noticing?

4. What boundary-setting experience are you most grateful for, even (and especially) if it was challenging? How has it helped you grow?

5. Imagine your wisest, most boundary-full future self looking back on this moment with pride and appreciation. What would they say to celebrate and affirm you?

Take your time with these reflections, and really let yourself savor the sweetness of your growth and progress. Offer yourself a silent (or spoken) "thank you" for showing up for yourself and your boundaries with such courage and devotion.

Part 2: Clarifying Your Growth Edges

Now that you've celebrated how far you've come, let's get curious about the boundary skills and situations that still feel edgy or challenging for you. Remember, identifying your growth areas is not about self-judgment, but self-awareness and self-compassion.

Consider the following prompts and write down your honest reflections:

1. What boundary-setting skills do you still feel less confident or comfortable with? Where do you tend to get stuck, frustrated, or discouraged?

2. Are there any specific relationships or situations where boundaries feel particularly tricky for you? What beliefs, fears, or patterns might be getting in the way?

3. When you imagine yourself setting and upholding boundaries with even more ease and grace, what inner resources or support structures would help you get there?

4. If you could wave a magic wand and change one thing about your relationship to boundaries, what would it be? What would feel different in your life as a result?

5. What loving message does your boundary-setting inner wisdom have for the part of you that still struggles or doubts? What compassionate encouragement do they most need to hear?

Allow yourself to be honest and vulnerable in this exploration. Trust that naming your growth edges is an act of self-honoring, not self-abandonment. By bringing awareness to the places where you still feel tender or tentative, you're planting seeds for your next stage of boundary development.

Part 3: Setting Your Boundary Intentions

Now that you've reflected on both your victories and your growth opportunities, let's turn our attention to the future. What intentions do you want to set for your ongoing boundary practice? What commitments do you want to make to yourself and your relationships?

Consider the following prompts and write down your heartfelt responses:

1. Fast-forward six months from now. What do you want your relationship to boundaries to look and feel like? What will be different in your inner world and your outer actions?

2. What specific boundary skills or tools do you want to practice and strengthen in the coming weeks and months? Which ones feel most aligned with your growth edges and goals?

3. How do you want to show up for your loved ones' boundaries? What kind of boundary-honoring partner, parent, friend, colleague do you want to be?

4. What support structures or accountability buddies will help you stay committed to your boundary practice, even when things get tough? Who can you reach out to for encouragement and guidance?

5. Craft a boundary mantra or affirmation that captures your highest vision and intention. Something you can come back to again and again to anchor and inspire you. For example: "I honor my sacred yes and no with clarity and compassion, and I invite others to do the same."

Let these intentions be both aspirational and achievable. Aim high enough to stretch and inspire you, but not so high that you feel overwhelmed or discouraged. Remember, the goal is progress, not perfection. Every tiny step you take towards more boundaried living is worthy of celebration.

Part 4: Keeping the Conversation Going

Congratulations, dear one. By completing this reflection, you've taken a powerful step towards integrating and personalizing your boundary learnings. But of course, the journey doesn't end here.

Boundary-setting is a lifelong practice, one that will continue to evolve and deepen as you do. There will be moments of triumph and moments of struggle, times when your boundaries flow with ease and times when they feel impossibly heavy.

Through it all, remember that you're not alone. You're part of a growing global community of boundary-setters, each doing their own brave and beautiful work.

Keep reaching out for support and inspiration, whether it's through therapy, coaching, workshops, or heart-to-heart conversations with kindred spirits.

And keep coming back to your own inner guidance, again and again. Trust that your boundary wisdom is always available to you, even in the most challenging moments. Listen for the quiet voice of your intuition, and let it lead you back to your truth. As you continue on your boundary journey, here are a few suggestions for keeping the conversation alive:

- Schedule regular boundary check-ins with yourself, using this Tune-Up Checklist as a guide. Notice what's shifting, what's sticking, and what new insights are emerging.

- Share your boundary victories and challenges with trusted friends or loved ones. Celebrate each other's progress and offer compassionate support in the sticky spots.

- Keep a boundary journal where you can process your experiences, track your growth, and record your a-ha moments. Let it be a safe space to explore the full range of your boundary-setting journey.

- Seek out boundary-related resources (books, podcasts, articles, workshops) that resonate with your current growth edge. Let yourself be nourished and stretched by fresh perspectives and ideas.

- Look for opportunities to be a boundary ambassador in your communities. Model clear and compassionate boundary-setting, and invite others into the conversation. Remember, every ripple counts!

Above all, keep coming back to the core truth that your boundaries are a sacred gift—not just for you, but for everyone whose life you touch. Every time you honor your yes and your no with clarity and compassion, you're contributing to a more boundaried world. A world where all of us can thrive in the fullness of our being.

CONCLUSION: THE BOUNDARY BALANCE: KEEPING THE LOVE STRONG

Here we are, at the end of our journey together. Or perhaps, more accurately, at the beginning of a new one.

Over the course of these pages, we've explored the transformative power of boundaries in our lives and relationships. We've discovered that boundaries are not walls to keep people out, but bridges to invite true intimacy and respect in. We've learned that saying "no" with clarity and compassion is one of the most profound ways to say "yes" to our own needs and desires.

Most importantly, we've come to understand that boundaries are an ongoing practice, not a one-time destination. Like any muscle, they require regular exercise and stretching to keep them supple and strong. They ask us to show up, again and again, for the sacred work of honoring our own and others' sovereign truth.

As you embark on this lifelong boundary journey, here are a few key lessons to carry with you:

1. **Your boundaries are a radical act of self-love.** Every time you set and uphold a boundary, you're sending yourself the message that your needs matter, that your desires are valid, that your truth is worth protecting. You're planting a flag in the ground of your own inherent worthiness.

2. **Boundaries are not selfish, but self-full.** They are not about pushing people

away, but about creating the conditions for healthy and mutually nourishing relationships. When you take responsibility for your own needs, you free others to do the same. Boundaries are a gift to yourself and to all those whose lives you touch.

3. **Boundary-setting is a skill that can be learned and strengthened over time.** It's not about getting it perfect, but about staying curious and committed. Every boundary conversation, every moment of self-honoring, every courageous "no" and heartfelt "yes" is a step towards greater mastery. Trust that you are exactly where you need to be in your own unique boundary journey.

4. **You are not alone in this work.** Setting and upholding boundaries can feel scary, vulnerable, and downright countercultural at times. But know that you are part of a growing global community of boundary-setters, each doing their own brave and beautiful work. Reach out for support, share your stories, and let yourself be nourished by the collective wisdom and resilience of your boundary brothers and sisters.

5. **Your boundary-full voice is needed, now more than ever.** In a world that often confuses worthiness with productivity, that celebrates self-sacrifice over self-care, that prioritizes profit over people and planet—your unapologetic "yes" and your compassionate "no" are revolutionary acts. Every time you choose to honor your own limits and desires, you are part of creating a more equitable, sustainable, and loving world for all.

As you continue to walk your boundary path, remember that progress is not linear. There will be days when your boundaries flow with ease and grace, and days when they feel clunky and impossible. There will be moments of exhilarating clarity, and moments of confounding confusion. Through it all, keep coming back to your own inner compass. Keep listening for the quiet wisdom of your "yes" and your "no."

And when you stumble or struggle (as we all do), remember to treat yourself with the same compassion and care you would offer a beloved friend. Speak to yourself with kindness, remind yourself of how far you've come, and recommit to your practice with gentle determination. Your boundary journey is unfolding in its own perfect timing and rhythm.

As we close this chapter together, I invite you to take a moment to reflect on your own boundary journey so far. What have been your proudest moments of boundary-setting? What new edges are you excited to explore? What support do you need to keep growing and thriving in your practice?

Consider setting a regular date with yourself—perhaps once a month or once a season—to check in on your boundary work. Reflect on what's going well, what's feeling challenging, and what intentions you want to set for the road ahead. Treat this time as a sacred appointment with your own boundary-full truth.

And as you go forth, dear one, know that you are infused with a love that is big enough, mature enough, strong enough to hold and honor all your vibrant yeses and your vital nos. A love that wants nothing more than for you to bloom in the full expression of your being, boundaries and all.

May you always trust and treasure that love as your most faithful companion on this boundary-full path. May it be the soft and steady ground underneath your brave boundary steps, now and forever.

With infinite faith in your journey & spirit wink,

Jeff

APPENDIX 1: SCRIPTS FOR STICKY SITUATIONS

Setting boundaries in the moment can be challenging, especially in situations that catch us off guard or trigger old patterns of people-pleasing. Having some ready-to-use scripts in your back pocket can help you feel more prepared and empowered to honor your limits and needs in the face of pressure or pushback.

Below are some sample scripts for common boundary scenarios. Feel free to adapt them to fit your own voice and circumstance. Remember, the key is to communicate your boundary clearly, calmly, and with as much compassion as you can muster.

Scenario 1: Declining an invitation without over-explaining.

Script: "Thank you so much for the invite, but I won't be able to make it. I hope you have a wonderful time!"

Scenario 2: Asking for space in a relationship.

Script: "I really appreciate our connection, and I'm also feeling a need for some more alone time to recharge. Can we talk about finding a balance that works for both of us?"

Scenario 3: Saying no to a request to borrow money.

Script: "I care about you and I want to be supportive, but lending money doesn't work for me. Is there another way I can help out?"

Scenario 4: Setting a boundary around communication during work hours.

Script: "I wanted to let you know that I'm trying to be more focused during my workday. Going forward, I'll be keeping my phone on silent and will respond to non-urgent messages at lunch or after work. If there's an emergency, please call me directly."

Scenario 5: Expressing a sexual boundary.

Script: "I really enjoy being intimate with you, but [specific act] is outside of my comfort zone. Can we explore other ways to connect that feel good for both of us?"

Scenario 6: Addressing a hurtful comment.

Script: "When you said [hurtful comment], I felt really [emotion]. I know you probably didn't intend to hurt me, but I need you to know the impact it had. Can we talk about how to communicate more carefully with each other?"

Scenario 7: Asking for more equitable distribution of household chores.

Script: "I've been feeling overwhelmed with managing the household lately. Can we sit down and come up with a plan to divide up the tasks more evenly? I'd really appreciate your partnership on this."

Scenario 8: Declining a request to take on additional work responsibilities.

Script: "I appreciate you thinking of me for this opportunity, but my plate is really full right now and I won't be able to take on any additional projects. Let's touch base again if things shift in the future."

Scenario 9: Asking for family members to call before visiting.

Script: "We love spending time with you, and it would work better for our schedule if you could give us a heads up before dropping by. How about we set up a standing monthly dinner so we can make sure to have quality time together?"

Scenario 10: Setting a boundary around unsolicited advice.

Script: "I know you care about me and want to help, but when you give me advice without me asking for it, I feel like you don't trust my judgment. I'll definitely reach out if I need your perspective. In the meantime, could you just listen and support me as I figure this out?"

Remember, these scripts are just a starting point. The most authentic and effective boundary communication will come from your own heart and experience.

As you practice using these scripts (and creating your own), pay attention to what feels good and what feels challenging. Notice any patterns of resistance or discomfort that come up for you, and be extra gentle and compassionate with yourself in those moments.

Over time, setting boundaries will start to feel more natural and intuitive. You'll develop your own unique boundary language—one that feels true to who you are and what you need.

Until then, keep these scripts handy, and don't hesitate to lean on them as you build your boundary muscles. Every boundary conversation, no matter how imperfect, is a step towards greater self-love and relational clarity.

You've got this. Keep showing up, keep using your voice, and keep honoring your sacred yes and no. The world needs your boundaried heart, now more than ever.

Appendix 2: Journaling Prompts for Boundary Discovery

One of the most powerful tools for boundary discovery is journaling. By taking pen to paper (or fingers to keyboard) and letting your thoughts flow freely, you can access deeper layers of your own truth and wisdom.

Below are some thought-provoking journaling prompts to help you explore your personal boundaries. Use them as a starting point for self-reflection, and feel free to let your writing meander wherever it needs to go.

Remember, there are no right or wrong answers here. The goal is simply to get curious about your own inner landscape, and to let your authentic boundary truth emerge in its own time and way.

1. What does the word "boundary" mean to you? What images, feelings, or associations come to mind?

2. Think of a time when you felt your boundaries were respected and honored. What did that feel like in your body? What did it allow you to experience in the relationship?

3. Now think of a time when you felt your boundaries were crossed or violated. What sensations arose in your body? How did it impact your sense of safety and trust in the relationship?

4. What are some of the messages you received growing up about boundaries? How have these messages influenced your boundary-setting (or lack thereof) as an adult?

5. What are your biggest fears or concerns when it comes to setting boundaries? What do you worry might happen if you assert your needs and limits?

6. What are some areas of your life where you feel your boundaries are strong and clear? What has enabled you to set and maintain boundaries in these areas?

7. Conversely, what are some areas of your life where your boundaries feel fuzzy or porous? What makes boundary-setting challenging in these domains?

8. Imagine your wisest, most boundaried self. What do they know about boundaries that you're still learning? What advice would they give you?

9. What would your relationships (with yourself and others) look and feel like if you were setting and upholding boundaries with more ease and consistency? Describe in detail.

10. Complete the sentence: "I give myself full permission to..."

11. Complete the sentence: "I release the need to..."

12. What is one small boundary you could set today that would make a big difference in your well-being? What support do you need to follow through?

13. Imagine everyone in your life respected and honored your boundaries perfectly. What would be different? How would you feel in your mind, body, and spirit?

14. What is your personal "boundary mantra"--a short phrase you can repeat to yourself when you need to bolster your boundary backbone?

15. Fast-forward to the end of your life. What do you want to be remembered for in terms of how you treated yourself and others? How can boundaries help you create that legacy?

As you explore these prompts, be gentle and patient with yourself. Boundary work is deep soul work, and it can bring up a lot of emotions, memories, and revelations.

If you find yourself feeling overwhelmed or activated, take a break. Reach out for support if you need it. Remind yourself that you're doing brave and important work, and that your boundary journey is unfolding in its own perfect timing.

Most importantly, keep coming back to the page. Keep showing up for your own boundary truth, even (and especially) when it feels challenging. Trust that every moment of self-reflection is planting seeds for a more boundaried and beautiful life.

APPENDIX 3: RESOURCES FOR CONTINUED GROWTH

Setting and maintaining healthy boundaries is a lifelong journey, one that requires ongoing learning, support, and inspiration. Below are some curated resources to nourish and guide you as you continue to grow in your boundary practice.

Remember, there is no one "right" path to boundary mastery. Trust your intuition to guide you toward the resources that resonate most deeply with your current needs and stage of growth.

And as you explore these offerings, keep coming back to your own inner knowing. Let the wisdom of others be a complement to, not a substitute for, your own boundary truth.

Books

1. "Boundaries: When to Say Yes, How to Say No to Take Control of Your Life" by Henry Cloud and John Townsend

2. "Set Boundaries, Find Peace: A Guide to Reclaiming Yourself" by Nedra Glover Tawwab

3. "The Art of Everyday Assertiveness: Speak Up. Set Boundaries. Say No. Take Back Control. Get What You Want." by Patrick King

4. "Boundary Boss: The Essential Guide to Talk True, Be Seen, and (Finally) Live Free" by Terri Cole

5. "The Power of a Positive No: Save The Deal Save The Relationship and Still Say No" by William Ury

6. "When the Body Says No: The Cost of Hidden Stress" by Gabor Maté

7. "Nonviolent Communication: A Language of Life" by Marshall B. Rosenberg

8. "Codependent No More: How to Stop Controlling Others and Start Caring for Yourself" by Melody Beattie

9. "The Dance of Anger: A Woman's Guide to Changing the Patterns of Intimate Relationships" by Harriet Lerner

10. "Daring Greatly: How the Courage to Be Vulnerable Transforms the Way We Live, Love, Parent, and Lead" by Brené Brown

Articles

1. "10 Way to Build and Preserve Better Boundaries" by Psych Central

2. "How to Set Healthy Boundaries: 10 Examples + PDF Worksheets" by PositivePsychology.com

3. "6 Steps to Setting Boundaries in Relationships" by The Gottman Institute

4. "A Guide To Setting Boundaries at Work" by The Muse

5. "10 Way to Set Healthy Boundaries with Toxic People" by Psychology Today

Podcasts

1. "Unlocking Us with Brené Brown," especially episodes on boundaries, vulnerability, and shame resilience

2. "The Boundaries.me Podcast" with Vicki Tidwell Palmer

3. "The Codependent No More Podcast" with Michelle Farris

4. "Beyond Bitchy: Mastering the Art of Boundaries" with Vicki Tidwell Palmer

5. "Therapy Chat" with Laura Reagan, especially episodes on boundaries and people-pleasing

Websites & Online Courses

1. The Boundaries.me Website and Membership Community

2. The Terri Cole Boundary Bootcamp

3. The Centre for Nonviolent Communication (NVC) and NVC Training

4. The DBT-CBT Workbook: Setting Boundaries and Assertiveness section and worksheets

5. The Brené Brown "Living Brave Semester" Online Course

Supportive Communities

1. Codependents Anonymous (CoDA) Meetings and Resources

2. Al-Anon Family Groups Meetings and Resources

3. Adult Children of Alcoholics (ACA) Meetings and Resources

4. Emotions Anonymous (EA) Meetings and Resources

5. Local Boundaries Workshops and Support Groups (search online or ask a therapist for recommendations)

As you navigate these resources, remember to pace yourself. Boundary work is not about achieving perfection overnight, but about committing to a lifetime of learning and growth.

Be patient and compassionate with yourself on the journey. Celebrate your victories, learn from your missteps, and lean on your support system when you need a boost.

Above all, trust in your own resilience and resourcefulness. You have everything you need to create the boundary-full life of your dreams. These resources are simply here to remind you of your innate wisdom and worthiness.

So keep shining and nourishing your body, mind, and spirit with the tools and teachings that help you thrive. And know that with every step you take, you are part of a global community of boundary-brave souls, all walking each other home.

PLEASE CONSIDER LEAVING A REVIEW

Hello there!

As an author, I know just how important reviews are for getting the word out about my work. When readers leave a review on Amazon or any other book stores, it helps others discover my book and decide whether it's right for them.

Plus, it gives me valuable feedback on what readers enjoyed and what they didn't.

So if you've read my book and enjoyed it, I would really appreciate it if you took a moment to leave a review on Amazon. It doesn't have to be long or complicated - just a few words about what you thought of the book would be incredibly helpful.

Thank you so much for your support!

Jeff

Also By

Our catalog is constantly growing!

Visit AdultingHardBooks.com

For our other titles and free bonuses!

www.ingramcontent.com/pod-product-compliance
Lightning Source LLC
Chambersburg PA
CBHW071323150726
47997CB00002B/586